YOU SHALL KNOW THE TRUTH

the power of adoration and proclamation prayer

*This book is dedicated to Bob Hartley, Bob Fraser and Gregg and Shelley Dedrick.
Without you, it would not even exist.*

Scripture quotations, unless otherwise noted as "ESV", "NKJV" or "AMP" are taken from the New American Standard Bible, Copyright © 1960, 1962, 1963, 1968, 1971, 1972, 1973,1975, 1977, 1995 by The Lockman Foundation Used by permission. (www.Lockman.org)

Scripture quotations marked "ESV" are from The Holy Bible, English Standard Version (ESV), copyright © 2001 by Crossway, a publishing ministry of Good News Publishers. Used by permission. All rights reserved.

Scripture quotations marked "NKJV" are taken from the New King James Version®. Copyright © 1982 by Thomas Nelson, Inc. Used by permission. All rights reserved.

Scripture quotations marked "AMP" are taken from the Amplified® Bible, Copyright © 1954, 1958, 1962, 1964, 1965, 1987 by The Lockman Foundation. Used by permission. (www.Lockman.org)

Scripture quotations marked "NIV" are taken from the THE HOLY BIBLE, NEW INTERNATIONAL VERSION®, NIV® Copyright © 1973, 1978, 1984, 2011 by Biblica, Inc.® Used by permission. All rights reserved worldwide.

You Shall Know The Truth

© 2014 – Ben Woodward – www.benwoodward.com

ISBN-10: 149222538X

ISBN-13: 978-1492225386

For questions about reproduction of this book for bible study, teaching or devotional purposes, please contact us via www.benwoodward.com. This book is copyrighted but parts of it may be reproduced with permission from the author.

0 2 4 6 8 9 7 5 3 1

www.benwoodward.com

Introduction

Writing a book wasn't exactly what I set out to do. This journey began when I was asked by a friend to create an audio CD of prayers for a project that he was working on.

As I thought about how to do this CD of music and prayer, I realized that I needed to explain why I pray the particular way that I pray. Without explanation, the way I pray can come across as pretty intense. I wanted to help people get a grasp on the "why" behind this type of prayer.

Initially, I wrote a short book called "The Power of Proclamation." I taught a few seminars on it, and people seemed to really respond to the ideas in the book. One man told me that it was "life-changing." That motivated me go back and reread what I had written! I wanted to find out what he was talking about!

After going over the original material, I began to see that the concepts needed further fleshing out. If what I had written was really impacting people, then I wanted to be able to give them the full picture. That was the origins of this book.

I don't really consider myself a writer. I am more of a songwriter than a book writer. But what I like to do is make things practical and easy to understand. This book was written with that in mind. All I am trying to do is explain my own journey of prayer and tell you the things I have learned. I am just one normal guy telling another normal guy or girl what I have seen along the road. I hope this book reads like a conversation and not like an essay. I hope that you feel like we are journeying together.

My journey has been complicated and difficult at times. It has been full of unanswered questions and situations that I could not explain without God. But in the midst of this journey, I began to learn a model of faith and prayer that sustained me and gave me a hope I could not have imagined in my life. This is not pie in the sky stuff. This is a real, practical tool to help you move beyond the lies you have believed about God and enter into a life of hope and truth.

I have tried to make the concepts as simple as possible. I wanted to make sure that any believer in Jesus could take this book and run with it. I hope that I have been somewhat successful. Most importantly, I have seen the concepts in this book transform lives. I know it can do the same for you.

The development of this tool for prayer is thanks to the encouragement of a few people who need to be mentioned.

My wife and children are the best family a man could ever have. We have the most amazing life! Although my passionate prayer life has been the result of overwhelming obstacles that we have faced, I am grateful to my wife who always points me back to the things that I have said over the years. She still makes me lie down on the floor and declare the goodness of God.

My friend and mentor Bob Hartley helped lay the foundation for adoration, proclamation, thanksgiving and supplication prayer in my life. His model of prayer has helped me dramatically change the way I think and provoked me to develop this tool. The concept for this model of prayer is a result of his years of faithfulness and the years he gave to living a life of adoration.

A different Bob, Robert Fraser, was the initial motivator behind this project. After spending five years leading worship for marketplace conferences with Bob, I was encouraged to take the proclamation prayers I was praying and turn them into a useful tool for people in all arenas of life.

Lastly, I have to honor my friends Gregg and Shelley Dedrick. For years, they have championed the gift of God in me and have challenged me to produce a practical tool that both explains and equips the "regular Joe" with the tools needed to live a life of adoration and proclamation prayer. They believed in me years before anybody else saw it. They were able to see the diamond in the rough and had the patience to chip away until I grew more refined. You can check out the wonderful work they do at www.ironbellministries.org.

I believe this book will enable you to get free from the lies you have believed about God and enable you to walk in truth. I believe the tools in this book will change your life. I have seen it happen over and over again. Understanding the power of adoration and proclamation prayer changed my life. I pray that it changes yours.

Ben Woodward

Special thanks to Jessica Dedrick, Bridgette Millar, Anna Mae Althen and many others who read through and edited the many various versions of this book. Your advice was invaluable.

"Prayer is not asking. Prayer is putting oneself in the hands of God, at His disposition, and listening to His voice in the depth of our hearts."

Mother Teresa

"We have to pray with our eyes on God, not on the difficulties."

Oswald Chambers

"Is prayer your steering wheel or your spare tire?"

Corrie ten Boom

Contents

Preface - Is there any hope?... 13

War all around us.. 17

As a man thinks... 23

The Truth... 33

Faith is the atmosphere of heaven 43

Adoration prayer... 53

The results of Adoring... 67

Trials produce perfection... 73

Your will or my will?.. 85

Beholding and becoming..95

Your Word is like a hammer... 103

The power of Proclamation..109

The answer to your unanswered prayer... 115

How to pray Adoration and Proclamation prayers................................ 119

Alphabetical attributes of God.. 121

Proclamation Example... 129

Adoration Exercise.. 133

Personal Exercise..134

Resources..135

DON'T GO ANY FURTHER JUST YET!

This book is designed to be used in conjunction with online interactive tools to help you pursue a deeper walk with Jesus, cultivate an abundant prayer life and walk out a daily life filled with hope.

To help you in this journey, we have developed online tools that accompany this book. So, before you start reading, go to:

www.benwoodward.com/truthstudy1

Enter the password "truth" to watch the first video: "Is There Any Hope?" before you begin reading the next few chapters.

Preface

Is there any hope?

In 1927, the submarine USS S-4 (SS-109) was accidentally rammed by the Coast Guard destroyer Paulding with the loss of all hands. The story that is relayed about the incident is gut-wrenching.

Paulding stopped but after lowering lifeboats, found only a small amount of oil and air bubbles in the water. Rescue and salvage operations began — only to be thwarted by the onset of severe weather. After a period of time, six survivors were discovered still trapped in the forward torpedo room. As the trapped men used the last of the available oxygen in the submarine, a diver placed his helmeted ear to the side of the vessel and received this Morse code message, "Is ... there ... any ... hope?"

Any objective observer of modern society would say we are in troubling times. It may be too drastic to say we are shipwrecked, but at the very least, we are taking on vast amounts of water. With an increase in violent crimes, mass shootings, unpredictable weather patterns and deteriorating relational connections, many people are feeling shipwrecked. We look at our lives, our finances, our future, society, the economy and any multitude of issues, and we feel hopeless.

To add to this already desperate situation, our prayers seem to be unheard and unanswered. We cry out in desperation for things to change and nothing does. Loved ones die of disease, bankruptcy takes place, addiction continues to devastate lives, and difficult situations remain difficult. God seems silent. It seems like we are knocking on the hull of our sunken ship asking the same question:

"Is ... there ... any ... hope?"

To have any chance of answering this question, we first have to decipher what is meant by the word "hope."

The modern definition of hope sounds something like this:

I hope you're feeling better soon.
That's what she hoped would happen.
Everyone in your family is well, I hope.
I hope I get into school.
I hope I don't get a cavity.
I hope I haven't bored you so far.

Modern hope is a concept that has no fixed address. There is nothing concrete about it and certainly nothing to really hold onto. It is a concept that is based on circumstance. The definition of hope is vague and insubstantial.

"A feeling of expectation and desire for a certain thing to happen."[1]

I have often used the word "hope" to mean the same thing. I wanted something to happen, but I had no idea if would actually happen or not.

Natural hope may or may not have a strong foundation, and may exist only as a feeling, or mental attitude. This hope gives us a reason to go on, based a notion that the desire can be achieved. Natural hope then is based on the natural. Natural reasoning, convincing as it may seem to be, is not an absolute guarantee. In this world, a good result is never absolutely guaranteed. [2]

Often, hoping for something leaves you disappointed and confused. You were hoping for a job promotion but someone else got promoted instead. You were hoping to get into that certain prestigious university but had to settle for a

---

[1] http://oxforddictionaries.com/us/definition/american_english/hope
[2] http://hopefaithprayer.com/hope/what-is-bible-hope

local community college instead. You were hoping for a big Christmas bonus but you were given a gift card to Starbucks instead.

Hope, however, remains a powerful and influential force. People cling to it while it remains. They anchor their future to it. Then the day comes when they are accidentally rammed. Tragedy strikes, circumstances change, and they drown in disappointment.

Hope that was once so tangible is lost. And yet the Bible defines hope very differently:

Hope does not disappoint us. Romans 5:5

If we define hope like the world defines hope, there is every reason to believe that hope *will* disappoint. But the Bible tells us that hope does not disappoint. Are you as confused as I am? It seems that the biblical idea of hope is remarkably different from the world's idea of hope:

And now these three remain: faith, hope and love. 1 Corinthians 13:13

Hope seems strangely out of place in this verse. I can accept that love is an eternal reality because I know that "God is love"[3] and as He is eternal, so love must be eternal. I can reason that faith is an eternal reality because Scripture tells me the "just shall live by faith"[4] and even more importantly, "without faith it is impossible to please God."[5] Faith and love seem to fit within the construct of what we consider to be eternal realities but how is "hope" an eternal concept? Isn't hope a temporary feeling until we receive the thing we hoped for?

It seems that our modern idea of hope is incongruent with the biblical idea of hope.

For hope to be an eternal reality, it has to be anchored to something that is eternal. Hope that is separate from God is not hope at all. The biblical idea of hope is a fixed expectation based on the promises of God in His Word. This type of hope is not based on what we know or do; it is based on who we know — Jesus. It is the guarantee that our expectations, if they are based on God's promises, will be fulfilled. This hope will endure. It is unshakable because it is based on the sure Word of God and the changelessness of God Himself.

---

[3] 1 John 4:8
[4] Heb. 10:38
[5] Heb. 11:6

Think about the things you have hoped for in your life. How many times have you have been disappointed because something did not happen as you expected? I would humbly submit that what you experienced was not hope at all, it was wishful thinking. If our hope is the worldly kind, then delay typically leads to despair. Despair often gives way to depression, which eventually leads to hopelessness. Because this kind of hope is not based on any real truth, there is nothing to hold onto until the answer comes. The person without the promises of God to hold onto is like a ship without an anchor in a stormy sea. For hope to be the kind spoken of in Scripture, it has to be anchored to the reality of who God is.

For many, hope had been placed in a specific prayer being answered in a specific way at a specific time. When the situation they hoped for did not materialize, hope was dashed and their trust in God was fractured. When you place your hope in an answered prayer, you ultimately set yourself up for disappointment when it doesn't happen.

Thankfully, God always has an answer to our unanswered prayer. He points at Himself — He is the answer. When you find Him, you find all the answers you will ever need.

But therein lies the real problem. We don't really know God like we say we do. If knowing God is the answer to all of our questions then not only do we need to know what God says about Himself, but we also need to know how to practically step into a life of hope based on this knowledge.

Many of us have places in our lives where hopelessness has crept in. We have dark areas of our hearts where the door to hope has been shut due to disappointment. Time and time again, I have watched as people I love have faced crisis in their lives and have been left without hope. I have put my ear to the hull of their sunken ship and made out the faint dots and dashes — *"Is ... there ... any ... hope?"*

Although the situation looks bleak, I can confidently say that there is hope. But getting there will require a fight. We can have hope, but are we prepared to do what it takes to obtain it?

1.

War all around us

We are at war.

This is not your average fight, though. There are no obvious front lines in this war. You may not be shot at, blown up or physically injured in this war, but you are at war nonetheless. Worse still, there is very little training for this kind of warfare because only a few even recognize that it exists. Most people go blindly throughout their day without any thought to it.

Our enemy, however, has built an arsenal of devastating weapons that he has targeted us with for years. Each day, he opens fire and does not relent in his blitzkrieg. Every day, we suffer from the effects of this unrelenting pressure. Yet, with all the arsenal of weaponry he has, he is very easily defeated. In fact, it is embarrassing how easily he can be defeated.

How do I know we are at war? The Bible tells me. It also tells me the nature of the war we are in:

For though we live in the world, we do not wage war as the world does. The weapons we fight with are not the weapons of the world. On the contrary, they have divine power to demolish strongholds. 2 Corinthians 10:3-4

We live in the world and that is an inescapable reality. Every day, I wake up, I open my eyes and the world is still there. If the first statement the Apostle Paul makes in this verse is true, then the second must also be true. The second statement, however, alludes to something that does not seem quite so apparent. Paul goes on to tell us that the war we are in is not fought with weapons such as the world has. There are no guns, no missiles, no Patriot Defense Systems. None of those weapons have the power to win the war we are in.

What is this war that we are in?

We demolish arguments and every pretension that sets itself up against the knowledge of God. 2 Corinthians 10:5a

> The war we are in is a conflict over the knowledge of God

The war we are in is a conflict over the knowledge of God. What is truth? Is God real? Does He really care about us? Why does He sometimes feel like a distant, uninterested third party? If He is interested, is He kind, or is He a dictator? Can He be trusted, or will He let us down?

Every day we are faced with questions like these in one form or another. Every crisis and every challenge we endure force us to ask the question:

Is God who He says He is?

This Is Not Your Typical War

Paul tells us that there are arguments and pretensions that try to force their way into our lives. These arguments are carefully constructed attacks to make us believe lies about God. *If we allow ourselves to believe these lies, then our circumstances will determine what we believe about God.* If our lives are going well then we will agree with the fact that God is good. If things are not, then God must not be who He says He is. When we live like this, what we see and what we feel will determine what we believe about the very nature and character of God.

This is not your typical war. This is attrition warfare. It is a constant barrage of noise designed to wear us down until we give up. It is the constant nagging in the back of our minds that we are not good enough, not doing enough, not wealthy enough and not righteous enough. It is every moment of every day! If we do not find the right weapons to fight back, we will have little chance of survival.

In my own life, I have encountered many situations that made me keenly aware of the type of war we are in.

I have a friend named Sharon* who recently went through a terrible divorce. Out of nowhere, after close to a decade of marriage, her husband decided he no longer wanted to be married to her. He walked out on her and left her with nothing. Sharon is young, beautiful and talented. This unexpected situation could have derailed her. What Sharon believed about God during that season would ultimately dictate the course of her future. Was God present? Did He care about her and her future? Did He have a plan for her future that was better than she could have dreamed?

A couple that is very dear to my wife and me were godparents to a little girl named Bailey*. Bailey was a beloved child born into a family that was unable to have children for 15 years. They prayed and prayed for years asking God to give them a child. One day, miraculously, the wife became pregnant. This was an enormous answer to prayer! Tragically, when this child was only 3 years old, she fell into a pool and drowned while the family was inside having a party.

Bailey was a beautiful little girl, adored by family and friends. She was an answer to the prayers of her parents. But at only 3 years old she was gone. How do you deal with a circumstance like this? What does this situation tell you about God?

Is God who He says He is? Does He really care about us, or is He a distant, uninterested third party? If He is interested, is He kind or is He a dictator? Can He be trusted or will He let us down?

Where Is God In Crisis?

My last example is a very personal one. One evening I received a message that one of my closest friends had been in a terrible car accident. He had been rushed to the hospital, and it appeared that he had been miraculously spared. A few days later I received a message from my friend in the hospital. The message said this:

"Hey, great to hear from you, surgery went well!! God has been all over this

*Actual Names Changed

whole ordeal. Thank you SO MUCH, for your prayers, love and support!"

Less than 24 hours later, he passed away in the hospital, his death the result of a pulmonary embolism.

You have to know a few things about my friend. He was in his mid-thirties, was married and had young children. Up until this point, he was a normal guy, loved Jesus, served as a worship leader at a large church and had no perceivable health issues. I was shocked by the news.

> In light of this situation, God, are you still who you say you are?

A few days later I got on a plane and flew across the country to attend his funeral. His life had such impact that close to 3000 people attended the ceremony.

As I stood over his cold body, many questions plagued me. How could this happen? Why did this happen? Where is God in this? I knew that, when the news had first gone out about my friend's death, a few people went to the hospital to pray for his resurrection. But here I was standing over his cold, lifeless body. I wept.

Days later, as I was taking a shower, I broke down again. I had so many questions. Why did he have to die? Why now? What about his family? As I tried to process through the pain, I realized that the main question I struggled with was this:

In light of this situation, God, are you still who you say you are?

I felt like I knew about God, but now I was faced with an unanswerable situation and realized that I wasn't as sure as I used to be. Had God changed? Or was there a deeper issue in me that had to be addressed?

I realized that my friend's death had exposed the truth about what I believed. God had not changed. He never will. But what I believed about Him was flawed. Somehow, I started to believe a lie about God that caused me to doubt Him. God is good, but somewhere, somehow, circumstances had found a way to cause me to doubt it. I was the victim of an assault on the character of God in my life.

Thankfully, I already knew how to fight this battle. This was not the first time I had been attacked in this war, and I am sure it won't be the last time.

What war am I talking about? *It is a war over the knowledge of God. What do I believe about Him, His nature and His character?*

This is a war that does not wait for you to be ready before the battle begins. It will come to you whether you like it or not. It will come after you in your marriage, your family and your relationships. This subtle but deadly war is raging in the lives of all of us every day. How, then, do we respond?

Our Weapons Have Divine Power

> We have weapons that enable us to fight in this war, and these weapons we have been given have divine power

Good news! We have weapons that enable us to fight in this war, and the weapons we have been given have divine power!

For the weapons of our warfare are not of the flesh but have divine power to destroy strongholds. 2 Cor. 10:4 ESV

This divine power is not of this world. If it was of this world, it would not be effective in this war. If the power to fight had to be summoned from within ourselves then we would very quickly lose. There is, however, a divine power and a supernatural grace that is available to tear down the lies that have separated us from the knowledge of God. This is not hocus-pocus or wishful thinking. This is very real divine power that is available to us right now.

We desperately need divine power. No person, however wise or educated, can answer the question of why Sharon's life is so difficult when the lives of others are easy. They cannot answer sufficiently why Bailey drowned at 3 years of age when other children have lived. They cannot answer why my friend was taken in the prime of his life leaving behind small children and a devastated wife. At the very best they can try to empathize but they will always fall short of answering the "why" questions.

Thankfully, there is a divine answer. Scripture tells us that there is a divine power to destroy every stronghold, every lie and every argument that come against the knowledge of God. While we may remain in the dark as to "why," we can answer the question of "who."

The divine answer is found in the character of God. To find this answer, we have to ask ourselves, "What do we really believe about God?"

2.

As a man thinks

I was born in New Zealand and raised in the wonderful nation of Australia. What this means, however, is that I experienced a little culture shock when I first moved to the U.S. Some differences were obvious. Americans drive on the wrong side of the road. They like everything supersized. They are incredibly patriotic. Certain things took a lot longer for me to adjust to. I still haven't found a good Aussie fish and chips restaurant yet!

My culture shock happened because I had ideas about America that were not the result of any actual experience. My perceptions of the U.S. were mostly the result of bad sitcom television and information I learned from tourists who visited Australia. The first time I flew into Los Angeles, however, everything changed. I crossed over from my secondhand knowledge to experiential knowledge. What I had only known from a distance, I began to know in reality. The problem is that reality is often very different from perception.

I love this passage from the author C.S. Lewis, *"What you see and what you hear depends a great deal on where you are standing."*[6]

Sometimes, what you think is true is far different from what is actually true.

---

[6] C.S. Lewis - The Magician's Nephew

Our circumstances, cultural heritage or even something as simple as our unique personality traits can distort our perception of what is true. The painful life lesson I needed to learn was that a "point of view" is simply that — a view from a point. As soon you move to a different point, the view becomes different.

Here is a perfect example. For thousands of years, people knew for a "fact" that the earth was flat (the Flat Earth Society still exists today although its numbers are few). That idea was ultimately debunked the first time somebody circumnavigated the globe. Experience (a real "knowing") will always expose thoughts and ideas that are actually only speculation.

In the Apostle John's gospel, Jesus is described as the *"Word of God made flesh."*[7] John used that description to tell us something about the nature of God. *He desired to be known!* This desire was so great that He revealed Himself in the flesh. Jesus was the physical expression of the very nature and character of God[8] and now, He was tangible. In fact, Jesus went as far as to say, *"He who has seen me has seen the Father."*[9]

> **Jesus was the physical expression of the very nature and character of God**

We use many words to describe things that we see, touch, taste or experience. These words alone, however, do not equate to actually having touched or tasted or seen.

John describing Jesus as the "Word made flesh" helps us to see what God's intention was. The very things that God had been trying to tell us throughout history — things about His character, His nature and His plan for creation — He now revealed in a flesh and blood body. This physical expression would enable us to access Him, relate to Him and know Him intimately. His desire was to restore to us the place that Adam had when he walked in the Garden of Eden and enjoyed communication, intimacy and friendship with God.

The Apostle Paul puts it eloquently like this:

For this reason I bow my knees to the Father of our Lord Jesus Christ, from whom the whole family in Heaven and earth is named, that He would grant you,

---

[7] John 1:14
[8] Hebrews 1:3
[9] John 14:9

according to the riches of His glory, to be strengthened with might through His Spirit in the inner man, that Christ may dwell in your hearts through faith; that you, being rooted and grounded in love, may be able to comprehend with all the saints what is the width and length and depth and height— to know the love of Christ which passes knowledge; that you may be filled with all the fullness of God. Ephesians 3:14-19

Paul makes it clear that all of the strengthening with might, all of the rooting in faith and all of the grounding in love are to help us to *know* the love of Christ. As we get to know His love, we will be filled with the fullness of God. Paul understood that it was not enough to simply know Scriptures about God; that knowing had to be translated into an experiential knowledge about God. This was the kind of relationship that God had planned for His people. Paul was inviting us to not just know about God, but to also experience God in His fullness!

> As we pursue the knowledge of God, He will come to us and demonstrate His character to us

The book of Hosea describes this same concept like this:

Let us know, let us pursue the knowledge of the Lord. His going forth is established as the morning; He will come to us like the rain, like the latter and former rain to the earth. Hosea 6:3

Hosea knew that the greatest journey we could ever go on would be a journey that allowed us to discover God. The pursuit of the knowledge of God would actually enable the releasing of His nature toward us. As we pursue the knowledge of God, He will come to us and demonstrate His character to us. This is an exciting invitation. When we, as followers of Jesus, take the initiative to pursue the knowledge of God, He will respond to us by releasing His character toward us. The result is an experience that enables us to be filled with the fullness of God.

Knowing God in a practical and relatable way was God's intention all along but many of us have been content with far less than what we have been offered. While we may agree to follow Jesus, few of us take the necessary steps to pursue Him and know Him as Paul wrote about to the Ephesian believers.

There is an interesting place just outside the earth's atmosphere where gravity is weak enough to keep satellites in orbit but not strong enough to pull them back to earth. The International Space Station (ISS) orbits in "low earth orbit" between 320 to 350 kilometers above the earth and has done so since 1998. Although you can live on the space station, it's probably not the most comfortable life.

I have a sneaking suspicion that many Christians live like the astronauts who reside on the space station. We are in an orbit of faith in Jesus, but we remain distant from experiencing the fullness of the "knowledge of the Lord." Although we may have enough faith to believe God for our salvation, we are hesitant to come any closer. This rudimentary knowledge about God may pull us into orbit around His Kingdom, but it will never allow us to enter into the fullness He desires for us.

Although many may remain content to stay that way, we were never created to exist perpetually in orbit. We were designed to fully experience all that God has offered us. But for us to walk in what Paul called the "fullness of God," our belief in God has to move beyond a rudimentary examination into an experiential knowledge of who He is.

The Way You Think Determines The Way You Live

The entry point is described by the wisest man who ever lived:

For as [a man] thinks in his heart, so is he. Proverbs 23:7 NKJV

The way a man or woman thinks will determine the way that he or she lives. This is a foundational truth that relates to everything we do in life.

What you believe in your heart about who you are and who God is will determine the way you live, move and have your being in this life.[10] If you believe that God is impatient with you and is just waiting for an excuse to punish sinful behavior, you will respond to God according to your perception. But, if you believe that God is a good Father who has your future in the palm of His hands, your response to Him will be remarkably different.

Your perception of God is critical in determining the way you think and respond to God. The issue is that most of us have false ideas about God that

---

[10] Acts 17.28

we think are true thoughts about God. Compounding those lies are various challenges that we have faced over time. These challenges reinforce the lies that we believe, causing us to respond in agreement with the lies. It's quite a mess, really.

This leads us to ask the question, "Where do these lies come from in the first place?"

Scripture is clear on this. We have a sworn enemy and his mission is to steal, kill and destroy.[11] But beloved, do not fear! We are partakers in the victory that was won over the enemy as a result of Jesus' death and resurrection. In fact, the purpose that Jesus came was "to destroy the works of the devil."[12] Jesus' victory gives us the confidence we need to realize that we have an enemy that is a defeated foe.[13] The weapon the enemy has left, however, he uses with devastating effect.

He lies!

The book of John gives us some compelling insight into the character of the enemy we face. In this passage, as Jesus is rebuking the Pharisees, we are given insight into the nature of our adversary:

> **Your perception of God is critical in determining the way you think and respond to God**

You belong to your father, the devil, and you want to carry out your father's desires. He was a murderer from the beginning, not holding to the truth, for there is no truth in him. When he lies, he speaks his native language, for he is a liar and the father of lies. John 8:44

The devil is not just a liar; he is the father of lies. Everything he does comes from his nature. This is his primary identity. When he lies to us, he is operating in his most natural form.

His lies plant the seed to bring forth sin in our lives. Although the devil may plant the seed, often the perpetuation of that sin is the result of our agreement with those lies. Although it is clear that that the enemy is a strong opponent, he needs very few weapons to accomplish his goals. He is fully aware of how

---

[11] John 10:10
[12] 1 John 3:8
[13] Revelation 1:18

powerful the weapon of deception is, and he uses it with devastating effect.

The Choice Is In Our Hands

Thankfully, we have some help on our side. When we realize that our adversary only has the power that we give him, he can be very easily defeated. But when we abdicate responsibility by not taking our rightful place as those who walk in the Spirit with a renewed mind, we allow the enemy's lies to take root in our lives.

The responsibility for the earth was not given to the devil and his demons. The authority to rule and the responsibility to oversee the earth were given to the sons of men.[14] Their mandate was to walk in the will of the God and, in doing so, release the Kingdom of the Father on the earth. If mankind continued in the will of God, then they would prosper. If they did not, then they would fall into sin, and subsequently death would reign over them. Adam and Eve's failure allowed a usurper to be in authority until the time of Jesus.

> When we abdicate responsibility by not taking our rightful place as those who walk in the Spirit with a renewed mind, we allow the enemy's lies to take root in our lives

But even after Adam and Eve fell into sin, man was still responsible to walk in the will of God and in doing so, bring life to the earth, even though they lacked the full capacity to do it.

We see this in God's statement to Cain in the book of Genesis:

If you do well, will you not be accepted? And if you do not do well, sin lies at the door. And its desire is for you, but you should rule over it. Genesis 4:7

Herein lies the issue. Cain still had the God-given authority and ability to rule over sin and not allow sin to rule over him. The responsibility for sin ruling in the earth is *in the hands of men and women*. Even though we recognize that the enemy lies waiting for a chance to ensnare us, we still have to actively

---

[14] Psalm 8:6

resist him or sin will rule over us. Once sin gets hold of a man or woman, they become ruled by it and live as a slave to its lusts. As a result, all kinds of evil are released in the earth because those called to resist did not take a stand against it.

Thank God for the new covenant of grace purchased by Jesus! As evidenced by human history, men and women always choose to live in sin instead of agreeing with the will of God for their lives. Humanity on its own could never return to the place of authority and partnership that was originally given to Adam. Only the victory accomplished in the death and resurrection of Jesus could give us a new Spirit-filled grace to accomplish what was previously impossible. We can now rule over it!

Knowing this, however, means that the problem of wickedness in the earth has as much to do with man's responsibility to rule as it does the deception of the enemy. The devil knows that, if he can convince you to believe a lie, you will perpetuate a life of sin on your own. The issue then is not just that the devil did it, but we agreed with him. All the enemy has to do is convince us to believe the lie and, when we do, we give him the authority he needs to keep us in darkness.

> Only the victory accomplished in the death and resurrection of Jesus could give us a new Spirit-filled grace to accomplish what was previously impossible

Oh, the enemy is exceptionally subtle with his lies. Most are not even aware that the lies exist in them. The lies are hidden deep under the camouflage of socially acceptable behavior and cultural acceptance. They are cloaked in bad theology and excuses. Don't be fooled, though! The lies are still there, and they must be dealt with swiftly and intentionally.

If you found out that you had cancer, the best hope you have for survival is to find out as early as possible and get appropriate treatment. The longer you are unaware of it, the greater chance it has to spread. Once it has begun to spread, your chances of survival are drastically reduced. So it is with the lies the enemy has planted in us about God.

The lies we believe about God are like cancer to our souls. They suffocate our hope and destroy our faith. They eat away at our confidence until there is nothing left but a hollow shell. But it need not be this way.

It's Not About What He Can Do, It's About Who He Is

If these lies are so destructive, then we have to find out what these lies are so we can deal with them quickly and effectively. What kind of lies are we talking about?

Most people believe that God can heal the sick. They could point to countless examples in Scripture and may have even heard of someone else being healed of sickness. Few believers have a problem with telling you that God can provide finances in a time of need. Most believers would boldly say that God is fully able to protect them in a time of danger.

But, if you ask that same believer if they think God would do it for them in the circumstance they are currently facing, more often than not, the answer would be, "I don't know." To save face, they might initially say yes, but often there is a nagging doubt that lingers in the recesses of their mind that says something like this:

"Sure, God can heal, but will He? Sure, God can provide, but will He? Sure, God can protect us, but will He?"

The issue is not a question of whether or not God can, *but whether or not He will do it for me.* This no longer becomes a question about God's ability, but a question about His character.

Is God who He says He is?

This is the type of war we are in. *This war is a conflict over the knowledge of God. What do I believe about His nature and character?*

This unbelief stands in complete opposition to the invitation to walk in the fullness of the will of God for our lives. Unbelief is not just a petty issue in the body of Christ that can be overlooked. Unbelief is a rampant disease that is unchecked and completely out of control.

The majority of besetting sins and issues in our daily lives can be pinpointed back to a lie or an accusation that we believe about the character of God.

Sometimes it is the product of circumstances in our lives that we have no control over. Sometimes, things happen that are not our fault. We have all had things that were not our choice and we were forced to endure crisis or abuse or disaster. It is typically in these moments that the seed of doubt is first planted.

I know God can, but will He do it for me?

Before you read the next few chapters, make sure you watch the second video: "The Truth Shall Set You Free." You can watch the video by going to **www.benwoodward.com/truthstudy2**, *entering the password "truth" and following the prompts.*

3.

The Truth

The Gospel of John tells us the story of the death of a man named Lazarus. Lazarus, Mary and Martha were close friends of the Savior, and this was a moment of family crisis that needed divine intervention:

Now a man named Lazarus was sick. He was from Bethany, the village of Mary and her sister Martha. (This Mary, whose brother Lazarus now lay sick, was the same one who poured perfume on the Lord and wiped his feet with her hair.) So the sisters sent word to Jesus, "Lord, the one you love is sick." When He heard this, Jesus said, "This sickness will not end in death. No, it is for God's glory so that God's Son may be glorified through it." Now Jesus loved Martha and her sister and Lazarus. So when He heard that Lazarus was sick, He stayed where He was two more days. John 11:1-7

Although Jesus was now aware of Lazarus' sickness, He did not immediately come. Instead, He delayed. During this brief time, however, Lazarus died. Mary and Martha were devastated. When Jesus finally made it to Bethany, everybody came out to meet Him — everybody, that is, but Mary.

You can hear the pain in the conversation between Jesus and Martha:

Now Martha, as soon as she heard that Jesus was coming, went and met Him, but Mary was sitting in the house. Now Martha said to Jesus, "Lord, if you had been here, my brother would not have died." John 11:20-21

Martha was hurting. Many of us have thought the same thing during times of crisis in our lives.

Lord, if you had been here when my husband walked out on me, if you had been here when my 3-year-old daughter headed toward the pool, if you had been here when my husband was breathing his last breath and dying from a pulmonary embolism ...

At the core of all of these questions is an accusation.

God, where were you when I needed you? Don't you care? I know you can do what is needed, but it's obvious that you don't care enough about me to do anything about it. I know that you can, but I'm not sure you will.

At least Martha came out to meet Jesus. Think about the emotion that Mary must have been feeling and the questions she would have had. Although Jesus was a close friend, she did not come out to meet Him when He arrived.

I thought you were our friend. You heal everybody else, but when it comes to your own friend, you let him die?

Finally, Martha must have convinced Mary to come out to talk to Jesus.

Then, when Mary came where Jesus was, and saw Him, she fell down at His feet, saying to Him, "Lord, if You had been here, my brother would not have died." Therefore, when Jesus saw her weeping, and the Jews who came with her weeping, He groaned in the spirit and was troubled. John 11:32-33

Jesus is once again faced with the same question. Although the question seems innocent enough, it implies a bold accusation against His character.

If you had been here ...

What they were really saying was *we know you can but for whatever reason, you weren't willing.*

This response caused Jesus such pain that it goes on to say that Jesus wept. I often ask people what it was that caused Jesus to weep. Did He weep because

He thought He might have missed it?

Maybe if I had just showed up a few days earlier ... Maybe I blew it this time. Whoops.

Was He weeping because He felt the loss of His friend? I really don't think that answers the question sufficiently. Jesus was about to raise Lazarus from the dead so it's unlikely He was weeping over a loss of friendship.

Jesus wept because the people who were His dearest and closest friends did not trust Him. Mary and Martha's words carried an accusation against His character. *If you had been here ...*

The Truth About The Lie

This is the same question that we often have during times of crisis. We know He can, but when He doesn't, or the situation seems too great, we let the circumstance become greater than God. Then we say the same kinds of things that Martha and Mary said. We accuse Him.

I wonder how many times the Lord has been moved by the words we have said or the accusations we have brought against His character? How many times has He wept over us? How many times in His love for us has He acted in our best interest only to have us accuse Him?

> A lot of people unknowingly believe lies about God but those lies show up clearest when they are faced with a crisis

Just like Mary and Martha, we do not question His ability; we just question His willingness.

A lot of people unknowingly believe lies about God, yet God has a tried and true method to bring these lies out into the open. He uses moments of crisis and difficulty. The lies always show up clearest when we are faced with a crisis. Do we really trust Him? Do we really know Him?

Causing humanity to doubt God's character and motive is a common attack of the enemy. Consider the enemy's first assault on the human race. His main attack was not to overwhelm Adam and Eve with hatred, lust or greed. All he did was accuse the character of God.

The third chapter of Genesis gives the account of the serpent attacking the credibility of God:

Now the serpent was more crafty than any of the wild animals the Lord God had made. He said to the woman, "<u>Did God really say</u>, 'You must not eat from any tree in the garden?" The woman said to the serpent, "We may eat fruit from the trees in the garden, but God did say, 'You must not eat fruit from the tree that is in the middle of the garden, and you must not touch it, or you will die.' <u>You will not surely die</u>," the serpent said to the woman. "For God knows that when you eat of it your eyes will be opened, and you will be like God, knowing good and evil." Genesis 3:1-5 *(Emphasis mine)*

> We know that God can do anything He wants to, but can He be trusted to do it for me?

You can hear the blatant lie and the accusation in the serpent's words. God is holding out on you. *He is not trustworthy. He isn't who He says He is.*

Eve's decision to eat the fruit spoke volumes about her trust in God's word. While we may not think we would do the same thing, it is easy to see where they stumbled.

This accusation against God is the same accusation the enemy uses today:

God is not trustworthy: He is holding out on you.

We know that God can do anything He wants to. He is God! But can He be trusted to do it for me?

The Power Of Unbelief

The enemy's successful attack on Eve has become the standard way the enemy has weakened the people of God throughout history. Plant the seed of doubt into the mind of a man or a woman and then let them speak it out until the doubt becomes unbelief. Water and fertilize that unbelief with difficult circumstances and hardship until it begins to form a mindset. The result is clear. Men and women who were designed to bear the image of God live locked up in fear. Those who were supposed to boldly bring the Kingdom of

God spend every moment concerned with their own self-preservation.

Unbelief has become a stronghold[15] within the church and because of its prevalence, we have accepted it as normal. To save face, we develop theology that protects us from the circumstances that we cannot control or understand.

Over the years, we have found countless creative ways to repackage unbelief so that it does not sound so offensive. We have labeled it "wisdom." We have found theological loopholes. We have justified it through personal experience.

The problem is that developing an incorrect theology about what God can or cannot do will never address the core issue. Repackaging unbelief in an acceptable form does not change anything other than making us feel better about it. What we must address is not our unbelief about God's ability but our unbelief about who God is.

We need to have our minds renewed to believe that God is who He says He is.

> **What we must address is not our unbelief about God's ability but our unbelief about who God is**

Many of us have allowed unbelief to be an acceptable sin that poisons our lives. The seed of doubt has now become a mountain of unbelief that needs to be spoken to and cast into the sea. To honestly address this unbelief will require us to take personal responsibility for the lies we have believed and then begin the process of uprooting those lies. Nobody else can do it for us; this journey is our own to take.

An Invitation Into Truth

There is an invitation for us today if we have eyes to see it and ears to hear it:

Let us pursue the knowledge of God ...[16]

Pursuing God will require us to change the way we think about God and start to agree with who He says He is. If our mind is the key to our behavior and responses, then changing the way that "a man thinks" will change the man.

---

[15] A place where a particular cause or belief is strongly defended or upheld. - http://oxforddictionaries.com/us/definition/american_english/stronghold?q=stronghold
[16] Hos. 6:3

In his letter to the Roman church, the Apostle Paul said:

And do not be conformed to this world, but be transformed by the renewing of your mind, that you may prove what is that good and acceptable and perfect will of God. Romans 12.2

It is clear. The transformation that is necessary for us to walk in the will of God must come from a renewing or a changing of the way we think. Paul says that when our minds are renewed, we actually prove that the will of God is good, acceptable and perfect.

The key to destroying unbelief is not gritting your teeth and hoping for the best but changing the way you think about God. This is not always an easy task. Past wounds, false identities placed on us by others, cultural acceptance and countless other factors hinder this transformation.

> **Unbelief may be a powerful force in our lives, but we have been given a simple solution to defeat it**

Unbelief may be a powerful force in our lives, but we have been given a simple solution to defeat it:

The truth.

Truth is our divine trump card. It is the divine weapon we have been given to wield in this spiritual war.

We are given a great example of what spiritual warfare looks like in the Gospel of Luke. This is one of the clearest demonstrations of the kind of struggle we face in our lives every day:

Jesus, full of the Holy Spirit, left the Jordan and was led by the Spirit into the wilderness, where for forty days He was tempted by the devil. He ate nothing during those days, and at the end of them He was hungry. The devil said to Him, "If you are the Son of God, tell this stone to become bread." Jesus answered, "It is written: 'Man shall not live on bread alone.'" Luke 4:1-4

It is entirely possible that I have watched far too many war movies, but I was expecting something a little more dramatic from what should be "The Battle of the Ages." Where is the "Lord of the Rings" epic battle? Where are the angelic armies, demonic hordes and exploding stars? This is Jesus and the devil out in the wilderness in the greatest battle of all time! But, alas, there are no crashing of armies, no war cries, no battle of arms. This was just a quiet conversation in the desert.

The entire spiritual wrestling match did not hinge on who could pull off the greatest miracle, sign or wonder.

Doubt was the key to the enemy's battle, but truth was the weapon of choice for Jesus.

Could the enemy cause Jesus to doubt who He was? Could the devil convince Jesus to doubt the Father's purpose for His life? Was the Father trustworthy or not? Let's look specifically at one of the temptations of Jesus:

> **Doubt was the key to the enemy's battle but truth was the weapon of choice for Jesus**

The devil led Him up to a high place and showed Him in an instant all the kingdoms of the world. And he said to Him, "I will give you all their authority and splendor; it has been given to me, and I can give it to anyone I want to. If you worship me, it will all be yours." Jesus answered, "It is written: 'Worship the Lord your God and serve Him only.'" Luke 4:5-8

Consider the subtle invitation the devil offers in this temptation. The enemy is trying to convince Jesus to bypass the will of the Father and take the easy way out. The enemy is whispering this lie:

"The Father is making this more difficult than it needs to be. There is an easier way. You can't trust Him."

How many times has the enemy tried to convince us of the same thing? There is only one way and it is through the cross! It cannot be bypassed. But the enemy will always try to convince us to take the easy way out.

Seeing how Jesus responded gives us a clue as to how battles are won in this war. Whenever Jesus was presented with an accusation or a question, He would not answer out of His own words or wisdom which, as the Son of God, would have been more than adequate. Jesus would only answer out of what was written in the Word of God. He would answer with truth.

For it is written ...

It is no wonder that Jesus declared this about the truth:

And you shall know the truth, and the truth shall make you free. John 8:32

The Truth Shows Us Who Jesus Is

The measure of freedom we have in this life is not related to our ability to do what we want. Our freedom comes as a result of understanding who God is and living according to His will.

> Jesus is the final definition of God's character and to pursue the knowledge of God is to pursue Jesus

Our true freedom and purpose comes when we live in agreement with the truth. *"I am the way, I am the truth,"* declared Jesus.[17]

Jesus was not telling us that He was *a* truth, or even a part of the greater definition of truth. He declared that He *was truth*. All that is true must come from Him and be found in accordance with who He is, or it is a lie. When we truly grasp the fullness of what this means, we can begin to take the courageous step of acknowledging that we have lived a lot of our lives in response to a lie. This will begin a journey of renewing our minds and aligning our lives with what God says.

Remember, Jesus is the full expression of God revealed to us.[18] He is "The Truth." If Jesus is the full expression of God's character, when we see Him, we see the fullness of God in a man. He is the practical, relatable and pursuable part of God. He is the final definition of God's character. To pursue the knowledge of God is to pursue Jesus.

We must address the lies we believe in our lives. Even though we have been saved, our minds are still full of things that contradict the truth of Jesus.

Counteracting these lies requires more than just determination. It requires a transformation. Although we must first see and acknowledge where we have

---

[17] John 14:6
[18] Heb. 1:3

missed it, to become free, we must have *a renewing of our mind.*

Our mind is the battlefield. The transformation we need in our lives will occur when we understand that "as a man thinks in his heart, so is he." We cannot walk in the fullness of all that we are called to walk in until we have our minds conformed to the mind of Christ.

When our minds come into agreement with who God is, everything changes. We are set free from the bondages that keep us back from walking in the fullness of the will of God. When our minds are renewed, everything becomes possible.

This is the war we are in. It is a conflict over the knowledge of God, the very nature and character of God. What do we believe about God? The last thing the enemy wants is for us to walk in the fullness of the knowledge of God. He knows that if we did, we would be unstoppable.

4.

Faith is the atmosphere of heaven

The war we are in is not a physical war; it is a spiritual war. We will, therefore, need spiritual weapons if we are to fight with any confidence.

In the Gospel of John, we read about a discussion Jesus had with a Samaritan woman that He met at a well. While there are many things that could be discerned from this conversation, there is one particular statement I want to focus on. Jesus made this emphatic declaration about God:

God is Spirit. John 4:24

Although talking about God being a spirit may seem obvious, it is a crucial piece of the puzzle that is often missed. This is a key that we must understand if we are to have any hope in this war.

God operates as a spiritual being. Therefore, for us to relate to Him, understand Him and walk in communion with Him, we must also understand something about ourselves. We are *spirit beings*.

Jesus alludes to this concept during another conversation He had with a man named Nicodemus. While discussing the nature of the Kingdom of God, Jesus makes this statement:

Unless you are born of the Spirit, you cannot enter the Kingdom of Heaven. John 3:5

This statement confused Nicodemus. How is a man supposed to be born again? Should he enter his mother's womb for a second time? But Jesus' statement was not about a physical birthing process but a spiritual one. Anyone who desires to be in communion with the Spirit of God must be born of the stuff that God is. It is impossible to enter the Kingdom of Heaven except a man or woman is born of the Spirit.

I have three children, and being involved in the birth of each one was both exhilarating and traumatic. There is nothing about birth that is clean or easy or comfortable. To phrase it like Jesus would, "Unless a child is born of the flesh, they cannot enter the kingdom of the world." A child that is born too prematurely has very little chance of survival. He does not have the capacity to live in the world. His skin, lungs and other organs are not developed enough to withstand the atmosphere of the planet. For a child to have the best chance to survive, he must mature sufficiently to be born of the flesh.

> Once we are born of the Spirit... we have access to the fullness of the Kingdom of God

In the same way, unless we are born of the Spirit, we do not have the capacity to function in the spirit realm. Once we are born of the Spirit, however, a wonderful thing happens. We have access to the fullness of the Kingdom of God!

Over time, we continue to grow and mature into a full understanding of the Kingdom of Heaven. We are not called to be immature. We are called to be fully mature spiritual citizens who function in the Kingdom of God as those who are natural to that realm.

A Spiritual Approach

We are not just natural creatures with a spirit; we are eternal spirits with a temporary fleshly home. When we become born again, we are not just our old selves with a "moral makeover," saved from sin and hoping to live a morally upright life. We are new creations — literally, a new species of humanity! Everything that is in Heaven is now accessible to us as creatures that are native to that realm.

To live in the world, I have to have a body that is able to function in the world's atmosphere. Our lungs are designed to breath a certain mixture of air that is found in our atmosphere. Our skin can only survive within a certain temperature range. Our bodies can only bear the weight that it is able to because of the unique force of gravity that our planet has. Just as our bodies are uniquely designed to function in earth's atmosphere, so our spirits are designed to function in a certain type of spiritual atmosphere.

The writer to the Hebrews gives us a glimpse into what that atmosphere is:

And without faith it is impossible to please God. Hebrews 11:6

Not possible.

Faith is the atmosphere of Heaven. Where faith exists, we are able to function as a spiritual being in God's Kingdom.

Faith is essential! Faith is not just something we need at a church service or a revival meeting. Faith is not just needed for the time when we really need healing or a financial breakthrough. Creating an atmosphere of faith is necessary for us to walk in a life of power.

> Faith is the atmosphere of Heaven. Where faith exists, we are able to function as a spiritual being in God's Kingdom

Our Christian life is designed to be more than just random moments of Heaven breaking out over natural circumstances. We should live every moment of our lives with a clear connection to a supernatural reality. An atmosphere of faith allows us to move from being supernaturally natural to naturally supernatural. That kind of faith is something that a lot of us have yet to experience, but it is the kind of faith needed to walk in the Spirit.

Faith Is My Proof

I love how the amplified version of the Bible describes faith:

Now faith is the assurance (the confirmation, the title deed) of the things [we] hope for, being the proof of things [we] do not see and the conviction of their reality [faith perceiving as real fact what is not revealed to the senses]. Hebrews 11:1

In 2013, I was in Sacramento with more than a thousand other foreigners who raised their right hand and swore allegiance to the U.S. After our swearing in ceremony, they handed us a piece of paper that was proof that we were now legal citizens. If anybody asks me if I am a U.S. citizen, I can now say, "Yes, I am." If they want proof, I can pull out my citizenship paper and show them the proof.

The writer to the Hebrews tells us that our faith is the proof of the things that we do not see. Our faith perceives as real fact the things that are not revealed to the senses. How do I know God is real? I have faith. It is my proof. How do I know my future is secure? I have faith. It's my proof. How do I know that I have a "new self" that has been made for me in the likeness of God?[19] I have faith. It's my proof.

> Faith does not have its certainty in the circumstance; faith finds its certainty in the nature and character of God

Although that may sound like doublespeak, it is actually a foundational reality that enables us to have unshakable confidence in God.

Faith does not have its certainty in the circumstance; faith finds its certainty in the nature and character of God. How can I believe things are going to happen even though reality would try to convince me otherwise? Because I have faith in God. This was the exact thing that Jesus encouraged His disciples to do.

Have faith in God. Mark 11:22

This faith, however, is not some kind of magical thing we use when we need it. It is not spiritual hocus-pocus. Faith is not something that is measured by what you feel but by who God is. Faith, then, is a necessary weapon that enables us to wage the war we are in.

Faith establishes an atmosphere where the spirit realm is alive and available because we trust in the character of God. How do we do that? By believing

---

[19] Eph. 4:24

that God is who He says that He is.

Growing up in the charismatic church, I heard the word "faith" used a lot. I have seen it used as a way to get rich and a way to get what you wanted. I have heard it as a catchphrase for certain movements within the body of Christ. I am not interested in anything that looks like "name it and claim it." The kind of faith I am talking about is a faith anchored to the character and nature of God, independent of the circumstances.

It's Not About How Much You Have

The difficulty with understanding faith is that we always try to measure it like we measure a cup of sugar (i.e., I need this much faith to believe for this). Thinking that way, however, shows how little we understand the concept of faith. Jesus, thankfully, addressed this idea.

One particular day, His disciples were struggling to cast a demon out of a boy. After Jesus rebukes the disciples for being part of an unbelieving generation and then casts out the demon, He gives this statement:

> **Our faith must be an agreement with who God is and what He desires to do**

Then the disciples came to Jesus privately and said, "Why could we not drive it out?" And He said to them, "Because of the littleness of your faith; for truly I say to you, if you have faith the size of a mustard seed, you will say to this mountain, 'Move from here to there,' and it will move; and nothing will be impossible to you." Matthew 17:19-20

Mustard seeds are small round seeds of about 1-2mm in diameter. Obviously, Jesus is not talking about a particular quantity of faith. Jesus was making a point. It's is not the size of your faith that matters; it's who your faith is put into that matters. The disciples were looking for a method when they should have been looking to God.

What kind of faith do we have? Faith is not a formula, a method or an incantation. Our faith must be an agreement with who God is and what He desires to do.

A lot of us look at our lives and don't see a whole lot of faith. We are faced with circumstances that seem to only produce doubt and unbelief. Thankfully, we are not the first people to look at a seemingly unchangeable situation and find very little to put our faith into. Ezekiel was faced with a similar situation as well:

The hand of the Lord was upon me, and He brought me out by the Spirit of the Lord and set me down in the middle of the valley; and it was full of bones. He caused me to pass among them round about, and behold, there were very many on the surface of the valley; and lo, they were very dry. He said to me, "Son of man, can these bones live?" And I answered, "O Lord God, you know." Again He said to me, "Prophesy over these bones and say to them, 'O dry bones, hear the word of the Lord.'" Ezekiel 37:1-4

While there may be very little we can do about the situation, there is something we can do about how we see the situation

When Ezekiel first looked at the dry bones, his response was "and lo, they were very dry." As Ezekiel looked, his natural eyes saw a situation that was unchangeable. *Immediately,* he was filled with doubt. The bones had been there a long time — so long, in fact, that the sun had bleached them white. It looked like this situation was never going to change.

A lot of people spend their entire lives living like this. They are ruled by what they see with their eyes. Often, the circumstantial evidence is overwhelming. They tell themselves, "This is the way it has always been and things are never going to change." They see a valley full of dry bones and "lo, they are very dry." While there may be very little they can do about the situation, there is something they can do about how they *see* the situation.

Is this an obstacle or is this an opportunity? What are you trying to do in this situation, Lord? If we believe that He is available and present in every circumstance then every situation, no matter how great or small, is an opportunity to discover God.

I find it interesting that the Lord asks Ezekiel a question about the bones. The Lord never does anything without purpose and this question had a specific purpose behind it:

Ezekiel, I know I am asking you to tell me what you believe about these bones but more importantly, what do you believe about me?

Ezekiel's response was to lean into God. I may not know how to answer the overwhelming finality of this situation, but I know you.

Faith At Work

God was intentionally creating an atmosphere for faith to come forth. Ezekiel, what do you believe? Ezekiel did not put his faith into whether or not the circumstance changed, he put his faith in God. That atmosphere of faith was the catalyst for Ezekiel to enter into partnership with God and see the dry bones come back to life. His faith may have been small, but it was faith nonetheless. It might have been just a mustard seed, but that was all that was necessary.

Often, when teaching these concepts, I will have people approach me with concern. Typically, they will make a comment like this:

"So, what you are telling me is that if I have faith, then the situation will change? Well, I tried that and nothing changed!"

> **Faith is the ability to have confidence in God regardless of the circumstances**

The type of faith I am talking about has very little to do with the situation and everything to do with what we believe about God. Faith must be anchored to who God is, regardless of whether or not the circumstance changes.

Having faith is not just an absence of doubt. Having faith means trusting God no matter what the circumstances say. We are not just devoid of unbelief. We are filled with something greater — a certainty that comes from God's character.

Sometimes, the circumstances don't change. Is God able? Of course! He is able to do whatever He desires. But do we believe He is willing? Do we believe He is for us even if nothing changes? Faith is the ability to have confidence in God, regardless of the circumstances. Faith perceives as real fact what is not revealed to the senses.

Even Jesus' ministry was affected by a lack of faith, as we find out from one story in the Gospels. Jesus came to a city that He was very familiar with but the results were unexpected:

And He did not do many miracles there because of their unbelief. Matthew 13:58

Jesus was a man full of faith and power. He had within Him all that was needed to accomplish the purpose of God. But because of their unbelief, He did not do many miracles there. The ability was there, but the atmosphere was not.

The kind of faith that was lacking in this example was not just a lack of faith about miracles (because He still did a few miracles there). The lack of faith was directly connected to what they believed about Jesus. A few verses earlier, we read about how the people of Nazareth had talked about Jesus:

When He had come to His own country, He taught them in their synagogue, so that they were astonished and said, "Where did this man get this wisdom and these mighty works? Is this not the carpenter's son? Is not His mother called Mary? And His brothers James, Joseph, Simon, and Judas?" Matthew 13:54-55

> **Faith perceives as real fact what is not revealed to the senses**

The people could not believe that the same little boy who had grown up with them could be a miracle worker. As a result of their lack of faith about who He was, He did not do many miracles there. It is astounding to realize the implications of a lack of faith in God. All that is available to us comes as a direct result of faith in God. Creating an atmosphere of faith has less to do with believing for a miracle and more to do with believing in the God of miracles!

We must remember that the ability to work is with God, not with us. We can agree with it in faith or disagree with it in unbelief, but the power still comes from God and must always point back to Jesus. We cannot hope to affect any eternal change outside of Jesus. Faith, in agreement with the will of God, the Word of God and the power of God always brings forth the work of God.

How we go about creating an atmosphere of faith is directly related to what we believe about God. Our faith is not circumstantial. Our faith is a by-product of our agreement with the character and the will of God. When we believe that God is real, available and willing, we become those who are able to function in agreement with Him. We start to operate as those who are "born of the Spirit."[20]

This spiritual birthing gives us the ability to operate with a new identity. As the Apostle Paul told the Ephesian church, we now have a "new self" created by God so that we might live in agreement with Him:

Put on the new self, which in the likeness of God has been created in righteousness and holiness of the truth. Ephesians 4.24

There is a new self that has been created in righteousness and truth for us. This new self is made in the likeness of God Himself. We become those who live in righteousness and truth. Although it is the work of the Holy Spirit to bring us to birth, we are called to actively participate by "putting on" this new self every day. How do we do that? Paul tells us a few verses earlier:

That you put off, concerning your former conduct, the old man which grows corrupt according to the deceitful lusts, and be renewed in the spirit of your mind. Ephesians 4:22-23

There it is again. *The answer is connected with a renewal of our minds.*

When I first began looking at this concept, it seemed too easy. There were no mountains to climb, no great journeys to attempt. I didn't have to take a vow of poverty and live in the desert or give up everything and go into the foreign mission field. Like me, your first impression might be, "Surely there must be something more I have to do." Well, it may not be as simple as it first appears. Changing the way you think can often be quite a battle.

The way we do this, however, is as simple as it gets. We follow the example of Jesus in the wilderness. We open our mouths and we speak out the truth.

---

[20] John 3.5

*Before you read the next few chapters, make sure you watch the third video: "Adoration Prayer." You can watch the video by going to **www.benwoodward.com/truthstudy3**, entering the password "truth" and following the prompts.*

5.

Adoration prayer

Jesus told His disciples an interesting parable in Matthew's Gospel about a farmer who sowed wheat in a field. While the workers slept, an enemy came and sowed tares into the farmer's field. A tare is a weed that looks like wheat but when it comes time for harvest, it produces nothing edible. It is sometimes called "false wheat." In the parable, the farmer allows both wheat and tares to grow together and be harvested together:

"The Kingdom of Heaven may be compared to a man who sowed good seed in his field. But while his men were sleeping, his enemy came and sowed tares among the wheat, and went away. But when the wheat sprouted and bore grain, then the tares became evident also. The slaves of the landowner came and said to him, 'Sir, did you not sow good seed in your field? How then does it have tares?' And he said to them, 'An enemy has done this!' The slaves said to him, 'Do you want us, then, to go and gather them up?' But he said, 'No; for while you are gathering up the tares, you may uproot the wheat with them. Allow both to grow together until the harvest; and in the time of the harvest I will say to the reapers, 'First gather up the tares and bind them in bundles to burn them up; but gather the wheat into my barn.'" Matthew 13:24-30

As we have been learning, the enemy's primary attack against us is to accuse the character of God. He sows the seed of doubt hoping that our agreement with it will produce the fruit of unbelief and sin. Just like the barren, unfruitful tares in this parable, the tares in our lives are ideas about God that often appear to be true but do not produce the harvest of righteousness in us.

The interesting thing is that God, just like the farmer in the parable, does not rush in and pull up the weeds. God allows the tares and the wheat to grow together. At times, it is difficult to understand why God would allow something to grow in our lives that could have such devastating consequences. Why doesn't God just step in and deal with it? As much as we would like God to bail us out of every situation that troubles us, He doesn't. He allows the tares to remain so that we are required to exercise our faith and take responsibility for what we believe. While the enemy may plant the tares, it is our responsibility to determine what remains.

For each of us, the tares sown into our life are uniquely designed to choke out the voice of truth. This doubt ultimately becomes a voice of accusation against the character of God.

> **God has designed us in such a way that our own voices can be used to defeat the lies of the enemy**

Sometimes these doubts are sown during a time of crisis or hardship. Sometimes they are sown during a situation in our life that we have no control over (e.g., abuse, neglect, physical illness or financial distress). During those moments, we are vulnerable and in pain. It is the perfect soil for the seed of doubt to be sown. The only thing that is needed for the tare to take root is our agreement with the lie.

Jesus describes the same principle in a different parable He gave to His disciples in the book of Mark. In this parable, the sower went out and sowed seed. As He sowed, some seed fell among the weeds and thorns. While that seed was still able to survive, it was never able to produce fruit. Jesus then went on to explain the meaning behind the parable. He said:

Still others, like seed sown among thorns, hear the Word; but the worries of this life, the deceitfulness of wealth and the desires for other things come in and choke the word, making it unfruitful. Mark 4:18-19

What a terrible thing to hear the Word and never apply it. What a waste it is to become unfruitful because of something like worry!

Where does worry come from? It is the product of our doubt. When we doubt that God is willing to take care of us, we begin to worry. Clearly, worry is directly connected to *what we believe about God*! If we do not address the weed (tare) of worry, it will choke our ability to be fruitful.

Doubt and lies are the enemy's weapons in the war. They convince us to live faithless, hopeless and godless lives. But the enemy's voice of doubt need not be the voice that determines our future. In fact, God has designed it in such a way that our own voices can be used to defeat the lies of the enemy, renew our minds and release the Kingdom of Heaven on earth.

Powerful Prayer

The book of James gives us a little insight into what that looks like:

The earnest (heartfelt, continued) prayer of a righteous man makes tremendous power available [dynamic in its working]. James 5:16 AMP

As we have already discussed, we have been given divinely powerful weapons[21] so that we may fight and win this war. James tells us that the power we are looking for is made available when we pray.

> **Prayer enables power to be released because prayer is the place that our voice finds agreement with God's truth**

Praying enables power to be released because prayer is one of the primary places that our voice finds agreement with God's truth. When we speak out what God has already spoken about Himself, we enter into agreement with the truth. When our voices are lifted in agreement with God, there are few more powerful forces on the earth.

Prayer is the vehicle that can bring together our faith and God's truth. But for many of us, this is not the type of prayer that we are accustomed to. This is a different type of prayer altogether.

---

[21] 2 Cor. 10:4

Let me tell you about a man I met years ago who became a mentor to me.

When I first met this man in 2006, he ran four businesses while also traveling and ministering across the world. He had a dynamic ability to equip marketplace believers with practical tools in prayer and hearing God's voice. Over the course of six years, I spent a significant amount of time with him as we traveled together, and I watched as he modeled a form of prayer that would become an essential tool for my life.

Because I had grown up in the church, I thought I knew how to pray. I knew how to open my mouth and say things that I thought were of value to God. But when I saw this man pray, I saw something completely different. I saw someone in love. And while I valued the history of prayer I already had, I wanted what I saw in this man — something authentic, dynamic and personal.

> He prayed like it was real and like there was a person who received his love on the other side

So over the course of time, he taught me how to pray a form of prayer he called "adoration prayer."

It seemed like an antiquated phrase when I first heard it, but it began to make sense when I experienced it personally.

The dictionary definition of adoration means "deep love and respect"[22] or "fervent and devoted love."[23] This was a pretty good definition of the type of prayer I initially encountered watching my friend pray. He prayed like a man in love. He prayed like it was real. He prayed like there was a person who received his love on the other side. He had a profound love and admiration for Jesus and his prayer was soaked in that love.

He would spend hours and hours in prayer. Although I had been in prayer meetings before, I had never experienced prayer like this. It was authentic and deep. I always left with a profound sense of the presence of God and knew that this was a man who lived out the command of Jesus to pray without ceasing.

---

[22] http://oxforddictionaries.com/us/definition/american_english/adoration?q=adoration
[23] http://www.thefreedictionary.com/adoration

I remember him telling me a particular part of his journey into this type of prayer. Years earlier, he had been invited to take on the role of youth pastor at a church in his hometown. Although he was a gifted communicator and a dynamic personality, the senior pastor of the church had a different plan for this young man's future. After accepting the job, he asked his boss what his job description was. The senior pastor told him, "I want you to spend three times a day in prayer."

That's it? Just pray? Surely there had to be more. He was ready to change the world but here he was relegated to the most boring thing imaginable — prayer.

He quickly realized that it's only possible to pray about your own needs for so long before you need to dig deeper. So he began to look in Scripture for the names and attributes of God and use that as a basis for his prayer.

What better way was there to defeat the lies I had believed about God than to use the very words that God had already used to describe Himself?

After months of praying this way, something changed inside of him. The God who he had been praying to became more than just a list of names and character attributes in an old book. He encountered a living, available, loving God. From that moment everything changed. He never wanted to leave that place of prayer ever again.

He would devour the Scripture to find out who God said He was and then he began to adore the Lord using the character attributes he had found. He would say that it was simply a person in love trying to show affection for somebody he loves. That gripped me. He once told me, "You can only tell your wife you love her so many times before she asks you if you have anything more to say."

Elizabeth Browning described this type of love in her famous poem:

"How do I love thee? Let me count the ways."[24]

---

[24] http://www.poets.org/viewmedia.php/prmMID/15384

This man began to document and alphabetize the attributes of God. He would stick note cards in his pocket so that when he worked, he always had a name of God to focus on.

It's Not Just About Obedience

Praying this way made sense to me in a different way. What better way was there to defeat the lies I had believed about God than to use the very words that God had already used to describe Himself? This would allow me to pray from a place of truth, basing my prayer on the actual nature and character of God.

As I began to adore the Lord, I quickly realized that this was more than just a way to understand the truth. This unique type of prayer was actually helping me to fall in love!

For years I thought that learning how to pray was just an issue of obedience. I genuinely thought that if I had more discipline or self-control then I would pray more. I thought that I just needed to get up earlier or stay up later, or somehow convince myself to just buckle down and do it.

> Everything was a way to both discover and connect with Jesus

Could you imagine a relationship like that? I have a wonderful marriage but I hope and pray that my wife actually wants to spend time with me. I certainly hope it's not something she has to discipline herself to do. I don't want her saying to herself, "If I can just be more disciplined, then maybe I would want to spend time with my husband." She wants to spend time with me because she loves me and knows me.

Maybe the reason I don't pray like I should is because I don't really know God like I think I do. Maybe my lack of desire to pray has less to do with discipline and more to do with my motivation. If we really knew Him, we would love Him and prayer would no longer be a chore but an invitation.

I realized that my friend had encountered a love so real that he couldn't help but pray. Everything he did, from his business, to his family life, his personal life and even his fitness[25] was lived out of the place of prayer. Everything was a way to both discover and connect with Jesus.

My life experience had taught me various methods of spirituality that helped me become a better Christian. I knew I was supposed to read my Bible. I knew I was supposed to go to church. I knew I was supposed to be morally upright and obey God's commands. These were all tools I had used to get me to my current spiritual maturity. But somewhere in me, doubts about God still remained. I had buried them deep, shoved them aside and tried to forget about them. But every time a crisis happened, the lies would come out as evidenced by my reactions and thoughts.

When finances were tight, I would start to fret. When my marriage was difficult, I would start to point the finger at my wife and get mad. Instead of trusting God and turning to Him, I turned to my own ability to find a way out. I knew this was not the right way to deal with the issues, but I wasn't sure how to change. I would immediately question God's goodness and faithfulness toward me instead of trusting Him and praying for His perspective.

Although I knew how to pray, I needed to be taught how to "pray through" (as my friend told me) so that, when hard times came, I would no longer question God's character. Adoration prayer taught me a different way to face my challenges. When things happened that I did not understand, I would respond with faith and prayer. I would adore the Lord and agree with His character. Unbelief was a bitter root, but I was discovering a way to dig it out.

> Adoration prayer taught me a different way to face my challenges. When things happened that I did not understand… I would adore the Lord and agree with His character

Teach Me How To Pray

Learning how to pray in a completely new way was humbling. But I felt a little better when I realized that even the disciples needed to be taught how to

---

[25] Over the years he and I traveled together, we stayed in many hotels. When we arrived at a hotel, he would have me come and work out with him at the fitness center. Our workout times consisted of prayer and adoration in between curls and lunges. You might think that is excessive, but it was the most normal expression of devotion for him.

pray:

It happened that while Jesus was praying in a certain place, after He had finished, one of His disciples said to Him, "Lord, teach us to pray just as John also taught his disciples." And He said to them, "When you pray, say: Father, hallowed be Your name. Your Kingdom come. Give us each day our daily bread. And forgive us our sins, for we ourselves also forgive everyone who is indebted to us. And lead us not into temptation."' Luke 11:1-4

The disciples probably felt a little inferior when it came time to pray in front of Jesus. Could you imagine praying in front of the Son of God? No pressure, but God is really listening now! In the course of their discipleship they had seen Jesus pray. They must have also seen something that they lacked so they asked Jesus to teach them how to pray.

Jesus consents and gives His disciples a concise and effective way to pray. We call this prayer "The Lord's Prayer," and many churches pray it verbatim to this day. Although the Lord's prayer has been dissected and discussed by people far more qualified than me, I want to focus on the first statement:

> **Jesus wasn't appealing to a distant God. He was praying to an approachable Father**

Father, hallowed be your name. Luke 11:2

Immediately, we learn something about the way Jesus prayed. Jesus wasn't appealing to a distant God. He was praying to an approachable Father. There were many titles that Jesus could have used when addressing God but He chose to use a title that represented family, familiarity and love. Basing His prayer on the foundation of God's character, He appealed to the glory of His name.

The entrance to a life of effective prayer is to first acknowledge who we are praying to and, in doing so, bring adoration to Him. This adoration is in direct connection to the majesty and value of His name. We don't begin with our list of demands and requests; we begin by appealing to His nature and His character.

This is what adoration prayer truly is. It is the entrance to a life of faith and truth by focusing on what God has said about Himself. It is allowing the Word of God to be the source of inspiration that helps us discover who God is. Then, in light of what we discover, we magnify and "hallow" His name. His name becomes the focal point of our prayer.

In the Old Testament, the names of God were a reflection of what He did and how He loved His people. He revealed Himself as a healer by declaring His name as *Jehovah-Rapha, the God who heals*[26]. He revealed Himself as a provider when Abraham called Him *Jehovah-Jireh, the God who provides*[27]. These are just two of countless character attributes revealed in Scripture. Adoration prayer focuses on character attributes like these. When we pray, we are literally praying the names God has revealed to us in His Word.

When teaching His disciples to pray, Jesus began with a focus on who God was and the holiness of His name. It was prayer based on an unshakable confidence in the nature of God.

There was a season when that kind of confidence was severely lacking in my own life. Although I believed God was good, I wasn't sure He was good toward me. I thought I needed to prove myself worthy of both His love and His favor. I did not pray from a place of confidence. I did not pray from a place of truth.

> **Adoration prayer focuses on the character of God by praying the names He has revealed to us in His word**

Have you found this to be true in your life at times? Do you also lack confidence in the goodness of God toward you? Are there areas in your life that you find it difficult to trust the character and willingness of God? Maybe you don't have a mentor like I did to help guide you but you do have the Holy Spirit! And now that you have the knowledge to be able to move forward in confidence, all that is left to do is apply the principles you are learning.

Adoration Prayer Changes The Way You Think About God

I began to discover a few things when I first started praying this "adoration prayer" method. As I used Scripture to pray, my mind was being transformed by the power of God's Word. My thoughts were changing day by day as I

---

[26] Ex.15:26
[27] Genesis 22:14

allowed the Word of God to not only be something that I read, but also something that I prayed. I realized that, *when I began to speak out* what God said about Himself, something shifted in my spirit. I began to believe it was true.

This did not happen immediately. Sometimes, I would pray things about God that I did not yet believe. *But as I continued to speak out* and thank God for what His Word said, it was as though the scales fell off my eyes. I began to see clearer and hear clearer. My mind was being transformed to believe what I was saying.

The result was remarkable. I began to fall in love with Jesus. As I stared into Him, I began to realize how wonderful He was. I began to see how much He cares for me and how great His love toward me is. I saw how He was always thinking about me, relentlessly working on my behalf and unconditionally loving me. When I saw how great His love is toward me, I couldn't help but love Him in return.

> When we adore God, we are saturated in His presence and filled with the word of the Lord

This changed everything. I used to think that prayer was something that I was required to do as a Christian. Now, it was different. Prayer became enjoyable. I was no longer presenting a list of requests to God while trying to twist His arm to do it. I wasn't even asking Him for anything. I was just telling Him who He was. I adored Him simply for who He said He was.

It's a simple but powerful principle. When we adore God, we are saturated in His presence and filled with the word of the Lord. Suddenly all our circumstances are seen in the light of who God is. The things that a moment ago seemed like mountains now become molehills. The impossible circumstances begin to seem possible. We discover the truth of what the Psalmist wrote when he said:

O magnify the Lord with me, and let us exalt His name together. Psalm 34:3

As I exalted His name, the battle all but disappeared. This biblical concept became reality during one particular time in my life.

The Day It All Made Sense

Early in my marriage, my wife and I worked for a prayer ministry. Although I am certain the ministry would have paid us if they could, they were very limited in what they could financially offer us. It became our responsibility to support ourselves financially while we worked with them. One particular night, I began to look at our bank account, and I realized that we were in an extremely precarious position. We had about one more month until the money ran out, and there was no income coming in the foreseeable future.

Many have been in a situation like this at one point or another in their lives. So I did what most would have done in that situation: I began to panic. Because of the impending catastrophe, I could feel the thick black cloud of fear begin to appear on the horizon of my life and knew that I had to make a choice.

I could give in to fear and worry, end up with stomach ulcers, have nothing change and still have no finances, *or* I could go into "fix it" mode and lean on my own strength to try to figure a way out of this mess, *or* I could get up, shake off the doubt, recognize where the enemy was accusing God's character and begin to adore the Lord as my provider.

> I was not going to leave this place until I felt a breakthrough, no matter how small

I chose to adore.

That night, I went into my office and began to pray into the character of God as Jehovah-Jireh, my provider. I reminded Him of His promise to always take care of us. I went through the Scripture and spoke to the Lord about all the times that He had come through for others. I continued to talk to Him about His nature until the cloud of doubt began to dissipate. I was not going to leave this place until I felt a breakthrough, no matter how small. When I received a sense of peace about the situation, I thanked the Lord and went to bed.

The next morning, I went to a local prayer room where we were living and I continued where I had left off the night before. I continued adoring the Lord and hoping in the character of God. I paced back and forward with a single desire — to stand on the Word of God that declared His faithfulness toward me. About an hour into my time of prayer, something changed.

I felt faith begin to arise in my soul.

The spiritual atmosphere in my life changed. Suddenly, my faith in God as a provider became the activating agent that set me on a course for a collision with Heaven. I knew my prayer had been heard and I felt like something shifted. Certain people would call it an encounter with God; others would have called it a divine revelation. All I knew was that something had changed.

Before I felt something change, I was reaching out for the promise of God just like you would reach out for a steady hand if you were falling. I was living in hope that I would catch that steady hand but I wasn't completely convinced I would. When the shift occurred, I suddenly began to feel the promises reach out for me. It was as though the hand that I was reaching out for now began to reach for me. Until this point, I was in pursuit of the promise of provision. Then I found and encountered a Father who loves me and cares about my needs. Now the promise was in pursuit of me.

> Adoration prayer is an entryway to a life of prayer and truth that enables us to discover who God is

It was an incredible feeling. At that moment, I realized the incredible power of adoration prayer. I realized that, as I began to speak out the true nature of God, a shift occurred first in me and then in the issues that were directly impacted by the character attribute I was declaring. I knew without a doubt that things were going to change.

That same afternoon, I headed home to find my wife waiting at the door with an open envelope in her hand and her mouth wide open in shock. We had just received an anonymous donation that covered our living expenses for three months! God had already answered our need before we even asked!

It's Not About A Formula, It's About Him

I wish I could say that this is a magic formula to get what you need in prayer. It is not because that was never the point. Although I have seen the Lord work this way many times, I have also prayed many times and nothing has changed. Nevertheless, by adoring Jesus in the middle of this difficult circumstance, I was able to access a level of faith and hope I had not experienced before. This faith and hope opened up the opportunity for the Kingdom of Heaven to be released in my life.

Adoration prayer is an entryway to a life of prayer that enables us to discover who God is. Remember, the battle we are fighting is not over the issue or circumstance in front of us. It is over the very name and character of God Himself. The enemy is trying desperately to convince us that the circumstances prove that God is not who He says He is.

The devil is at war with us to make us unfruitful and impotent. He knows that if he can get our eyes off God and onto the issues, then he will win the battle. The battle is not about the issue or circumstance; it is about the character of God. What do we really believe about Him?

Prayer enables power to be released in our lives. Prayer is the vehicle that can bring together our faith and God's truth. The most powerful way I have found to practically do that is through a model of prayer called adoration prayer. Adore God in truth and be amazed as you fall in love with Him and see Him for who He is. Let it stir up faith in you to defeat the lies of the enemy. Then stand back and watch as everything around you begins to change.

6.

The results of Adoring

Adoration prayer is a tool that enables God's truth to penetrate your mind, your heart and your life. Although there are many ways to pray, I have found a power in praying the character of God that cannot be matched. As you pray in agreement with God's Word, the impact on your life is remarkable. When you become anchored to Jesus, the Rock, you can weather any storm, face any obstacle and overcome any lie.

Although the results of praying in this way are immeasurable, the book of Psalms gives us some clear promises and outcomes from living a life of adoration.

1. When you adore the Lord, you *become a person with unshakable confidence*.

I have set the Lord continually before me. Because He is at my right hand, I will not be shaken. Psalm 16:8

Adoration allows you to set the Lord before you at all times. No matter where you are or what you are doing, you can stop and adore the Lord in that situation. When this becomes the default response, the circumstances no longer have control of your emotions. You are no longer ruled by what you see but by the truth of who God is.

There have been many times during my marriage where my wife and I will find ourselves in the middle of an escalating fight. What began as a simple disagreement has now turned into a firestorm. In those situations, I have learned that adoring the Lord changes the perspective of a room. When the situation gets too heated, we will stop, look at each other and begin to adore the Lord for who He is. This gets our eyes off the situation and onto Jesus. I wish I could say that this is what happens every time. It doesn't. Often, my pride will not allow it. But when I have the courage to lay down my pride and adore Jesus, things change.

> "Adoration" changes the perspective of a room

When you turn your eyes toward the Lord, things change. Adoration allows you to see with a different perspective.

2. When you adore the Lord, you are *brought into His protection.*

One thing I have asked from the Lord, that I shall seek: that I may dwell in the house of the Lord all the days of my life, to behold the beauty of the Lord and to meditate in His temple. For in the day of trouble He will conceal me in His tabernacle; in the secret place of His tent He will hide me; He will lift me up on a rock. Psalm 27:4-5

Adoration prayer brings you into God's protection. When the day of trouble approaches, God will keep you from faltering. This does not always mean you are protected *from* trouble, but you can have confidence that you are protected in the midst of trouble.

When Paul and Silas were locked in a prison cell for their faith, they begin to lift up their voices in song. As they sang, an earthquake released them from their chains, opened up the prison doors and set all the prisoners free.

Paul and Silas could have been dejected and depressed after being locked up in prison but instead they chose the path of adoration. As they adored the Lord, everything changed. The most beautiful part of the story is the salvation that came to the house of the jailers! Paul and Silas' adoration and song not only delivered them, but also delivered a whole household into the Kingdom of God!

3. When you adore the Lord, *you are delivered from fear.*

He delivers me from all my fears. I will bless the Lord at all times; His praise shall continually be in my mouth. My soul will make its boast in the Lord; the humble will hear it and rejoice. O magnify the Lord with me, and let us exalt His name together. I sought the Lord, and He answered me, and delivered me from all my fears. They looked to Him and were radiant, and their faces will never be ashamed. Psalm 34:1-5

> Adoration prayer keeps my mind focused on Jesus and keeps my mind in a place of peace. He delivers me from all my fears

Sometimes, if I am awake in the middle of the night, I suffer from mild anxiety attacks. Often my mind has trouble shutting off and the attacks come when I start thinking too intently about certain things that I can't explain. While I have always been puzzled as to why it happens, the anxiety I often feel is very real.

When these attacks occur, I get up out of bed and begin to adore the Lord. I begin to declare His nature as the God of Peace. I adore Him and turn my mind over to Him as the God who created my mind and understands how to keep me in perfect peace. I firmly believe that this is an attack from the enemy but I know that light and darkness cannot exist in the same place at the same time. As I adore the Lord, He brings peace and delivers me from fear.

Adoration prayer keeps your mind focused on Jesus and keeps your mind in a place of peace. He is the God who delivers you from all your fears.

4. When you adore the Lord, *you have access to overwhelming joy.*

In your presence is fullness of joy; in Your right hand there are pleasures forever. Psalm 16:11

Adoration allows your emotions to be determined by who God is and not by whatever circumstance you are facing. When you know who God is, you can't help but have joy! Jesus is the happiest person who ever lived. When you are around Him, you can't help but be happy. When you know that He has everything taken care of, you have no reason to despair. All your worries are turned into joy.

There was a time when my wife needed some dental work done. During this season, our health insurance deductible was very high and I knew that this work would cost us close to $1,000. One day, I came home and found myself frustrated by the thought of having to spend $1,000 on teeth. I would much rather spend that money on a vacation to the beach!

But, instead of allowing the circumstance to rule my emotions, I told my wife it was time to push the furniture aside and lay on the floor (that is our code word for a time of serious adoration). As we got down on the floor and declared His nature, we began to feel joy arise in us. We put on music, called the kids into the living room and danced! As we danced, the frustration disappeared and hope began to arise in us. Joy filled our home!

Was there a change in our circumstance? Not at that time because what we really needed was a change in our perspective!

Adoration brings you into a place of joy as you focus on who God is. Although the circumstance may not change, your perspective is shifted as you allow the truth to penetrate your heart and mind.

5. When you adore the Lord, *you become a light for others.*

He put a new song in my mouth, a song of praise to our God; Many will see and fear And will trust in the Lord. Psalm 40:3

I have taught the concepts in this book as a seminar in churches and groups all across the U.S. for many years.* Time and time again I get feedback from people who were radically changed by the seminar. The most common feedback I get is something akin to this:

"I loved the seminar, but when I saw you pray it all made sense. I knew what you were saying was true, but it wasn't until you prayed that I realized it was

---

If you are interested in bringing this seminar to your church or group, go to www.benwoodward.com and follow the links to contact him.

the life-changing tool I needed."

When you adore the Lord, you are able to bring light and truth into the lives of others. As we will discover, adoration transforms us into the image of Jesus. As we adore Him, we become more like Him. Adoration prayer not only helps us to see Jesus, but it also helps others to see Jesus.

There have been countless times when I have brought adoration prayer into a circumstance and it has helped others get a perspective of Jesus that they wouldn't have had by themselves. Adoration prayer is a game changer.

Fulfilling The Great Command

These are just a few of the powerful promises that come as a result of turning our eyes upon Jesus. But the single greatest thing that happens when we adore Jesus is that we fulfill the greatest commandment. We learn how to love Him!

"Teacher, which is the great commandment in the Law?" And He said to him, "You shall love the Lord your God with all your heart, and with all your soul, and with all your mind." Matthew 22:36-37

As we adore Jesus, we fall in love with Him. This is the single greatest reason why adoration prayer is so important. It enables us to see Jesus. When we see Him for who He is, we can't help but fall in love with Him.

This is the single greatest reason why adoration prayer is so important. It enables us to see Jesus and as a result, we fall in love with Him

God is looking for wholehearted lovers. He does not want just a portion of your heart or a portion of your mind. He is looking for those who will love Him with their whole heart, and their whole soul and their whole mind.

Adoration prayer is one of the greatest ways to enter into this command. It enables our hearts, souls and minds to be in agreement with God. As we agree with Him, we fall in love with Him.

For those of us (like me) who are romantically deficient, learning to love the Lord can almost seem like an insurmountable task. We have enough trouble remembering to buy our wives flowers! But learning to adore the Lord enables us to have a clear, definable entry way to fulfilling the great command of Scripture. Adoration gives us a new perspective of God and, as we gain this new perspective, we are also enabled to fulfill the great command to love Him with all our heart, soul and mind.

7.

Trials produce perfection

Learning how to adore the Lord in prayer opens up a whole new way of seeing life. When you discover who God really is, you also become aware of what He thinks about you. Suddenly everything begins to change. Now you have an invitation into a relationship with the God of the universe. He desires to partner with you and share His heart with you. This heavenly partnership is a mystery beyond comprehension. Jesus went as far as saying that because you are His friend, He shares everything with you. He has even given you the Holy Spirit to teach you, guide you and counsel you!

I no longer call you servants, because a servant does not know his master's business. Instead, I have called you friends, for everything that I learned from my Father I have made known to you. John 15:15

It is hard to comprehend the full truth of that statement. Jesus said that *everything* He learned from His Father He has made known to us — everything!

If we, as friends, are invited into such a depth of understanding about God that

He reveals His secrets to us, then that should change some things. But not only are we friends, we are a part of His church and called His bride! There are things that I will share with my friends but there are far deeper things that I share with my wife. The intimate details of my life are an open book for the wife who I love. I don't hold anything back, and there are no secrets between us. True, authentic relationship with another person demands nothing less.

Relationships are always built on a foundation of healthy communication. When that communication falters, then the relationship begins to suffer. Open up the lines of communication and you can begin to move forward.

Effective communication always requires humility, openness and time. Over the course of time, healthy communication changes from talking at each other to talking to each other. Once you learn how to do that, you can then begin the process of learning how to truly *listen* to each other. Eventually, you realize that healthy communication has far more to do with listening than talking.

> **Effective communication requires humility, openness and time**

When the lines of communication are open, you have the opportunity to discover who that person is. Love will always blossom when you discover the uniqueness of an individual. What would happen if we were given an opportunity to discover the uniqueness of Jesus and the untold riches of His glory and grace? It is this type of partnership and communication we are invited to enjoy with God.

Learning How To Love

I remember the early stages of falling in love with my wife. I always wanted to be around her. I would walk miles just to be near her, and one time I actually did. Love was a natural, unforced response.

When we first entered into our relationship, love was easy. Every word was like honey and every moment was like Heaven on earth. It was a blissful time, full of emotion and passion. This passionate love culminated in a marriage covenant. But after a few years of marriage went by, we started to have some difficulty. We had to work through differences of opinion, miscommunication and unrealistic expectations we had placed on each other. The love that was at first sweet, easy and tender was now faced with the realities of life and all its challenges. Now we were faced with a choice.

Do we give in to the difficulties and grow distant from each other? Do we view the challenges and messes we have made as reasons to give up or do we choose again to recommit to each other, now that we know what "love" truly means?

One day, as we were discussing the concept of godly marriage, a friend said this statement to me:

"Ben, first love is sweet, but second love is deep."

First love is tender and passionate. But second love is a choice. Second love is born of adversity and trial but carries with it the depth to last whatever storms may come. Second love is a decision made with a full understanding of the consequences and the responsibility that lie ahead. It is a recommitment to love.

> This testing of our faith is a divine set up to enable us to be perfect and complete in every way

This concept is one of the main reasons that adoration prayer is so important. When we go on the journey to pursue the knowledge of God, we discover who He is all over again. Second love is the real journey of walking in the knowledge of God.

When a person commits their life to Jesus for the first time, they are often clueless to what they are saying "yes" to. As time goes on, the choice they made is often tested by circumstances and trials of every kind. The Apostle James described it like this:

Consider it all joy, my brethren, when you encounter various trials, knowing that the testing of your faith produces endurance. And let endurance have its perfect result, so that you may be perfect and complete, lacking in nothing. James 1:2-4

This testing of our faith is a divine setup. It is designed by God to enable us to be perfect and complete in every way. It actually benefits us when we are faced with difficult circumstances that challenge our idea of who God is. It doesn't often feel like that at the time, however.

The Testing Of Our Faith

Although they did not understand it at the time, it was necessary for the Israelites to walk through the desert for forty years. After being delivered from Egypt, they knew very little about the God who rescued them. They had just spent four hundred years as slaves to the Egyptians crying out for the revealing of "God the Deliverer!" But for those slaves to become a nation like God intended for them, they had to face the hardship of the wilderness.

Only the wilderness could teach them about the God who supplies their need, the God who protects them, the God who is a healer and the God who is a lawgiver. Through the hardships they endured, they learned not just a first love for God, but also to choose to love Him all over again.

Many aspects of the character of God are only discovered when the winds of life are at their strongest. Just as a diamond cannot be formed without immense amounts of pressure, so it is with our lives. Just as muscles cannot grow without resistance, our spiritual lives cannot grow without trials.

> **The pressures of life and the circumstances allow us to grow deep in the knowledge of God**

Thankfully, the Lord has designed our lives in such a way that the pressure of life (if we are willing) will enable us to see the many faces of God displayed in every moment. Just as the winds and storms enable a tree to put its roots deep in the earth and become strong, so the pressures of life allow us to grow deep in the knowledge of God.

James tells us that we *must* face the testing of our faith if we are to complete. This means that we cannot hide from the difficult situations in our life. We must face them and allow them to reveal what is in us. We cannot run from the pressure when crises and trials come. We must stand and see the deliverance of God. Crises and trials will always come to us; however, it is our responsibility — as we are empowered by the Holy Spirit — to respond with biblical hope.[28]

When we face trials and hardship, we enter into a new season of relationship

---

[28] Gen 4:2

with the Lord. We begin to discover new things about Him that amaze us and captivate us.

Then, and only then, with a greater knowledge of what we are facing, can we say "yes" to Jesus all over again and enter into "second love." We can choose to love — not because of how it makes us feel emotionally, but because we are compelled by the character and nature of the One we are choosing.

But what happens when you are faced with circumstances that you didn't choose? What happens when you are forced into something you would have never chosen for yourself? What does that say about the character of God?

It's Not Your Fault, But Now It's Your Choice

I grew up in a family that did not have a lot of money. One particular house we lived in was right next to a railroad track. Every day we would hear the trains as they practically rolled right through our living room. As a child, I didn't know any different. I thought the way we lived was normal.

At times, we would eat things like creamed corn, canned spaghetti or baked beans on toast. I know, that's weird. One day, years after I was married, I decided to pull out a can of creamed corn and eat it with my toast. My wife looked at me like I was crazy.

"What are you doing?"

"I'm eating creamed corn on toast."

"Why?"

That was a good question. I didn't know why.

As I thought about it, I realized that my parents did not have a lot of money as I was growing up. More than likely, what we had for dinner was a can of whatever was in the cupboard poured over toast. That was normal to me but apparently not normal to my wife.

This "growing up poor" issue did not just relate to weird things I put on toast, however. I noticed that, the older I got, the more I became a penny pincher. I was constantly checking the balance of our bank accounts and berating my wife about what she spent our money on.

Without realizing it, I was allowing my circumstances to rule my emotions. This was not a conscious decision, however. It was the byproduct of circumstances I had no control over. I was responding the way I did because of a life I didn't necessarily choose.

More often than not, you don't get to choose what circumstance you end up in, but you do get to choose how you respond to it. Although it may not have been my fault that my parents were poor, it was now my choice to decide how I was going to respond to it.

A lot of people feel this way. We have situations and circumstances in our lives that we did not choose. Life is hard. Sometimes, it's harder than hard.

You finally pay off one credit card and the next day your car breaks down, needing thousands of dollars' worth of work. You finally recover from one illness only to have another disease cripple your health. Over and over, I hear the stories of people who feel like they can never get out of the pit.

But that's part of the problem. Often, we keep trying to get out of the situation, not realizing that it was the Lord who orchestrated the events that allowed us to be there in the first place. Sure, He could step in and save us from our temporary issues. But then we would never become the people He desires us to be. We don't realize that these circumstances are actually vehicles to enable us to discover who God is.

The questions you have to ask yourself are: What are you going to do with the circumstance you have been given? Will you curse God and die like Job's wife encouraged Job to do,[29] or will you take a stand and believe that, even though the circumstances may look one way, you are going to believe that God is who He says He is?

It's Not A Pit, It's An Opportunity

I told you that I grew up in a poor family. I recognized, as I got older, that I was being controlled by the fear of having no money. When I realized that the root of this fear was a lack of faith and belief in God as a provider, I began to declare His nature over my life. I could do nothing about my circumstances, but I had the power and authority to change my perspective and put my faith in the God who promised to provide for me.

---

[29] Job 2:9

Time and time again, I saw God move in my life with financial miracles. In one particular instance, I needed surgery but my health insurance deductible was quite high, and I was going to have to pay for the entire surgery out of pocket. At that point in time, I was working for a church on a reduced salary. My wife and I had no savings because the year prior to this, the Lord instructed us to empty out our savings for some friends in need. I was not sure how we were going to pay for the surgery, but I knew God.

One day, I came home frustrated after thinking about our situation. I told my wife that we needed to adore Jesus together because I was losing perspective. We pushed the furniture out of the living room, got down on the floor and began to read some of the prayers I had written about God being a provider (see the Adoration and Proclamation Prayer Book for more info on these prayers). We adored. We proclaimed His nature. We rejoiced. We declared who He was. We danced with our kids in the living room. Faith was rekindled. Hope was restored.

The next weekend I was preaching at our church. I told our congregation the situation and what we did in response to it. I wasn't telling them because I was hoping for someone to respond financially, but one member of our church family did. Someone wrote us a check for $1,000 because, in his words, "Isn't that what we do when there is a need?" Needless to say, I was stunned by that man's generosity.

> **We rejoiced in who He was. We danced with our kids in the living room. Faith was kindled. Hope was restored**

Three weeks later, I was preaching again at our church. During my message, I began to tell the story of this individual's generosity in relation to my family's need.

In the middle of sharing, a member of our congregation stood up and made his way toward the front of the room. Walking right up to me, he handed me $100 and then walked back to his seat. I was lost for words. But this was just the beginning. Over the course of the next thirty minutes, more than two-thirds of the room walked up to the stage and emptied their wallets on the pulpit. To this day, I have never experienced such an unprecedented, unprovoked response from a congregation. Without prompting, they gave. As we finally began to close the service, there was still a line of people waiting to give.

The result of this outpouring of love was that our financial need was more than covered. In fact, it was almost double the amount we needed. The most remarkable part of the story is that the amount we received was almost exactly equal to the amount that we had previously given to our friends a year prior.

Let me tell you this — you cannot outgive God! I was reminded again that the correct response in any crisis is to adore Jesus. Do not allow the circumstances to tell you who God is. Always respond by focusing on His character, and allow that to determine your response.

Every situation is an opportunity to discover God. It was never about what God could do for me. It was always about who He is to me. God is able to move on our behalf in a second. He has the capacity and the ability to dynamically shift our circumstances at any point in time.

> I have found that the key to my success is realizing that every situation is an opportunity to discover God

So, why do certain things remain the same no matter how long and hard we pray? Because God cares more about what is happening in your heart than in your hands. He is always after getting at the root of the disease: Will you trust Him no matter what the circumstances look like?

You have to learn to agree with God and not your circumstances. It's time to believe that God is for you. Become convinced that His thoughts toward you are always good, no matter what the situation looks like:

How precious also are Your thoughts to me, O God! How vast is the sum of them! If I should count them, they would outnumber the sand. Psalm 139:17,18

God's thoughts toward you are always good because He is good. Once you believe that, you can face any situation with confidence knowing that today is a part of the good plan of a good Father.

Have you ever stood on a beach and considered how may grains of sand there must be on that beach? Millions? Billions? If God's Word is true then His thoughts toward you are that vast and great. He has been thinking about you for eternity and every thought was good and every plan was perfect.

Every divine disruption in your life was the beautiful handiwork of God to make you more like Him and to set you up for a more glorious future than you could ever have imagined. Every random occurrence during the day and every slight misstep now become opportunities to discover God in the moment and encounter His love in a new way.

All that is left for you to do is choose to believe it.

It's easy to get frustrated by all the things that don't turn out like you expect them to. We always want to control the situation and manage the outcome. But God likes to surprise us! Even the seasons of life that seem like dark pits are opportunities to discover the goodness of God.

> Every random occurrence during the day and every slight misstep now become opportunities to discover God in the moment and encounter His love in a new way

I know that sometimes you don't feel like rising to the occasion. I know that sometimes it is easier to crawl back into bed and pretend like the world has disappeared. But that is exactly what the enemy wants you to do. He wants you to give up. He wants the circumstances to be so overwhelming that you throw in the towel.

During these times, you must remind yourself that every trial is simply an invitation to a deeper level of love and dependency. Every difficult thing you face is actually a doorway to a discovery of God. Every trial is a divine setup that enables you to enter into "second love."

The best thing you can do during times of trial is to open your mouth and declare the truth of who God is. Let the circumstances become a small thing in your eyes. Sometimes it will feel like your mouth is full of sawdust and you can't even speak. I remember many times in the past when I tried to proclaim the truth of God and it felt like my mouth was sown shut.

But I know that God's truth always trumps the situation, no matter how great it is. Remember what the Apostle Paul said:

We are destroying speculations and every lofty thing raised up against the knowledge of God, and we are taking every thought captive to the obedience of Christ. 2 Corinthians 10:3-5

Our minds are full of speculations and ideas that are set against the knowledge of God. The definition of "speculate" is to form a theory or conjecture about a subject without firm evidence. Our minds are full of theories about God that have absolutely no firm evidence. The evidence we need is found in the Word of God. But to change our minds, it must be spoken out of our mouths.

> While we cannot choose when we find ourselves in the pit, we can choose what we will do when we are there

Although we cannot choose when we find ourselves in difficult circumstances, we can choose what we will do when we are there.

Don't Go Through It, Go Over It

Years ago, I was flying in a small propeller plane with a friend of mine who was training to be a pilot. As we were flying, we were suddenly faced with a wall of cloud that was so dense that we could not see through it. While the instruments in the plane were useful to keep us upright, we could not see to navigate any longer. So my friend pulled back on the control yoke and we rose hundreds of feet in a matter of seconds. Suddenly we were over the top of the clouds and could see perfectly.

If you can't see where you are going, just get up a little higher. If the clouds are too thick, get above the clouds. Sometimes we think it is more courageous to just keep charging through the situation until we get to the other side. Instead, don't keep trying to go through it; go above it.

We cannot always escape the "pit" experiences in our lives but we have been given a tool that will enable us to fly above the clouds of despair. When we look at Jesus, we are lifted above the temporary issues and given a new perspective. We can suddenly see from 10,000 feet and it all becomes clear.

He is in control. He has my future in the palm of His hand. He is faithful to finish what He began in me. The Word of God promises us that we will face temptation and frustration. But it also promises a way of escape — not to get us out of it, but to enable us to endure it:

No temptation has overtaken you but such as is common to man; and God is faithful, who will not allow you to be tempted beyond what you are able, but with the temptation will provide the way of escape also, so that you will be able to endure it. 1 Corinthians 10:13

What an amazing gift we have been given. Bound up in the character of God is the power and ability to endure any crisis we may face. If we are willing to submit ourselves to His will and His plan, we will no longer be shaken by any circumstance we face.

The question is, are we willing to submit our lives to His will?

Before you read these next few chapters, make sure you watch the fourth video: "Becoming like Jesus." You can watch the video by going to **www.benwoodward.com/truthstudy4**, *entering the password "truth" and following the prompts.*

8.

Your will or my will?

I have a daughter who is four going on 14. She doesn't want help getting dressed, getting her food, drawing her pictures ... she pretty much doesn't want help with anything. She is independent. One morning, I was trying to help her get dressed when over and over she kept telling me, "I can do it, daddy, I can do it!"

After about 15 minutes with her head stuck in the wrong place, I decided to help her out. I pulled the shirt back off, put her arms through first and then pulled the shirt over her head. I appreciate that she desperately wants to do it herself but her independent spirit often gets her in trouble. A lot of us have the same problem.

All throughout the Old Testament, we have examples of men and women who tried to do things on their own. Abraham gave birth to Ishmael after he tried to fulfill God's promises through his own plans. Saul was removed as king over Israel when he tried to offer a sacrifice before Samuel arrived. David's plan to restore the Ark of the Covenant to Jerusalem was disrupted when Uzzah was killed. All these things could have been avoided if the lines of communication had remained open and these men had listened to the plan of

God. But the independent spirit is not easily overcome. We are far too self-reliant!

While we strive to prove our self-worth through our independence, God has a different plan for us. He desires to work in partnership with us. His whole plan is contingent on our partnership with Him. To facilitate this partnership, God invites us into His presence so that He might reveal to us who He is.

In the Old Testament, God gave Moses plans to build a tabernacle. This tent was specifically designed so that God might dwell among His people and speak to them:

Let them construct a sanctuary for me, that I may dwell among them. Exodus 25:8

Although that system worked for a while, it was not ideal. In the New Testament, God revealed who He was through the person of Jesus. He then placed His Spirit inside us so that He could dwell in us. Where the old covenant required a building to house God, the new covenant required a person:

Or do you not know that your body is a temple of the Holy Spirit who is in you, whom you have from God, and that you are not your own? 1 Corinthians 6:19

> God was not content to just live among us; He wanted to live in us!

This is a remarkable realization. God was not content to just live among us; He actually wanted to live in us! God's desire was for us to know Him, love Him and then partner with Him in redeeming the earth.

To remain in partnership with Him, we must remain in communication with Him. Prayer enables that communication to take place. It enables us to hear from Heaven about what God is doing and get divine wisdom for our lives.

Without that communication, we run around trying to accomplish what we think are the plans of God while never really understanding what the will of God is. Prayer is a way of intentional communication with God that gives us access to His plans. That intentional communication is the foundation to a healthy and ongoing partnership with God.

Having An Effective Prayer Life

To pray effectively, we have to understand the fundamental rule of an engaged and productive prayer life. When we pray, we are always praying for His will. This was one of the key aspects of the way that Jesus taught His disciples to pray:

Your Kingdom come. Your will be done, on earth as it is in Heaven. Matthew 6:10

God's will is what is important. It is His Kingdom that has priority, not ours. We are not trying to accomplish our will on the earth. We are establishing His. Our will, our plans and our lives became a secondary concern the day that Jesus called us to follow Him. We no longer have the right to determine our future or make any decisions outside of our relationship with Jesus. Whatever the Lord asks of us, we are bound by a covenantal relationship to lay down our lives for Him.

Although this may sound simple enough to understand, it is harder to pray. The reason this is so difficult is because the majority of our prayers revolve around our needs and concerns. Rarely do we stop and consider the question, "What does God want me to pray for?"

> **Rarely do we stop and consider the question, "What does God want me to pray for?"**

We spend countless hours praying for a certain issue and never once stop to ask the Lord if we are praying in the right way or not.

Many years ago, when the Internet was a new thing, I was in a touring band. My band had a website that a friend had developed for our music but it needed a few things updated. Although I had no experience building websites, I took it upon myself to not only update the information but also redesign the entire website. Nobody asked me to do it and I didn't ask anybody if I should do it; I just did it. I uploaded it to the World Wide Web and contacted the rest of the band to let them know what I had done.

Needless to say, it was not received well. Mildly put, they were mad. They were mad because I had not even consulted with them. I never asked them what needed to be done and now it was already on the web. Then I got mad because they didn't appreciate all the hard work I had put into it.

After a brief conversation, they contacted the original designer and he was happy to restore the website to its former design.

Although it is funny to look back and remember my youthful stupidity, I often catch myself doing the same thing when I pray.

This is what I want to happen, so I am going to pray and hope that God agrees with me and does what I think should be done.

While we may not always consciously think those things, we rarely take the time to follow Jesus' example and seek the will of the Father. This statement summed up Jesus' whole life and ministry model:

> **Jesus lived His life as a model for those who would follow in His footsteps**

Therefore Jesus answered and was saying to them, "Truly, truly, I say to you, the Son can do nothing of Himself, unless it is something He sees the Father doing; for whatever the Father does, these things the Son also does in like manner." John 5:19

It was the will of the Father that Jesus was concerned about. Even though He was fully capable as both God and man to operate out of His own initiative and desire, He didn't. In doing so, He set an example for us to follow.

He Is The Firstborn

This is an important truth to take hold of. Jesus lived His life as a model for those who would follow in His footsteps. The apostle Paul, in his letter to the Romans, used an interesting phrase to describe Jesus:

For those whom He foreknew, He also predestined to become conformed to the image of His Son, so that He would be the firstborn among many brethren. Romans 8.29

Jesus is the *"firstborn among many brethren,"* meaning that He is the example that we are to follow not just by partaking of His death but also by *partaking of His life*. We have access to the same Holy Spirit that Jesus did when He walked the earth. Because of that access, we have the capacity to walk as Jesus did. This doesn't make us Jesus, but it does mean we are supposed to look a whole lot like Him.

The only way that this can become a reality is when we, like Jesus, live in agreement with the will of God.

Now it is important to make a distinction here. I am not talking about understanding the exact purpose and plan of God for every situation. I am, however, talking about God's will. Jesus prayed that "God's will" would be accomplished. While we strive to pray for and understand "the plan" of God, the far more important thing to pray for is His will.

Why am I making a distinction between God's will and God's plan? Because although it is true that we should seek to understand the plan of God, sometimes it can be difficult.

The plans of God are often complicated, and they rarely make sense to our human understanding. If God had told Joseph about His plan to have him sold into slavery and then thrown into prison, I am not sure that Joseph would have agreed to the journey. If God had told the children of Israel about the 40 years that they were going to spend in the desert, I'm not sure they would have left Egypt.

> His will, however, is understandable and relatable because His will is always an extension of His character

The plans of God can often be confusing and frustrating. His will, however, is understandable and relatable because His will is always an extension of His character.

God's will was that none should perish[30] and, as a result of His will, a plan was set in motion. The plan of God was to send Jesus to be crucified because it was an extension of His character as the God who is love. It is not a plan that we would have understood before it took place, but we understand it now. Even the disciples had difficulty with that plan.[31]

But we can understand the will of God if we know His character.

I no longer question whether or not I should pray for the sick because I know

---

[30] 2 Pet. 3:9
[31] Matt. 16:21-23

the character of God as a healer.[32] I do not always understand the plan of God, but I do know the will of God. I may not understand why certain people get healed when others don't, but I will still pray believing that He is a healer. I certainly don't understand why some have to have surgery while others are miraculously healed but it doesn't change my response. I may not understand the plan of God but I do know the will of God so I will always strive to pray in agreement with His will.

This has been the case countless times in my life. On many occasions, I had to stand on what I knew was the will of God, because I knew what the Word of God said about His character. Although the situation or circumstance often seemed to say otherwise, I stood firm on the truth and prevailed.

> **Knowing His will is vitally important when we pray. It gives us a framework upon which we can build our life and walk in partnership with God**

Knowing His will is vitally important when we pray. It gives us a framework on which we can build our life and walk in partnership with God. Finding the will of God means that we must go on a journey of pursuing His character because His will is an extension of His character. Lester Sumrall defined it this way, "The Bible refers to God by many different names, and each one reveals some aspect of God's character or His relationship with us."[33]

To understand the will of God we must first find out the character of God. God has given us great insight into His character by declaring both His name and His character to us throughout Scripture.

Aligning Ourselves With God's Will

When Moses asked to see the glory of the Lord on the mountain, God revealed His name.

Then Moses said, "I pray you, show me Your glory!" And He said, "I myself will make all my goodness pass before you, and will proclaim the name of the Lord before you ... Then the Lord passed by in front of him and proclaimed, "The Lord,

---

[32] Psalm 103:3
[33] Lester Sumrall – The Names of God – Whitaker House

the Lord God, compassionate and gracious, slow to anger, and abounding in lovingkindness and truth." Exodus 33:18-19; 34:6

This is a key moment in history. Since Adam and Eve's departure from Eden, God had hidden His glory from mankind. This was the first time since then that God openly displayed His glory to a human. But what Moses saw was not what any of us would have expected.

God declared His name.

The revealing of the glory of God would happen again in the life of Jesus. But again, what they saw was not what they expected. Jesus' life revealed the character of God.

Jesus said that He had declared the name of God to His disciples through the way that He lived.

O righteous Father, although the world has not known you, yet I have known you; and these have known that you sent ye; and I have made your name known to them, and will make it known, so that the love with which you loved ye may be in them, and I in them. John 17:25-26

Adoration prayer directs our focus toward the name of God and away from our issues

Adoration prayer directs our focus toward the name of God and away from our issues. As we pray the name of God, we discover the character of God and subsequently the glory of the Lord is revealed to us. As we continue to pray, we become those who are in agreement with His character. This brings an alignment to our lives that we did not have before.

I have a friend who is a chiropractor, and I see him about once a week so that he can adjust and align my spine. One day he was describing to me what was taking place in my body. He told me that because of the nature of our busy lives and the effects of trauma to our bodies, our spine often gets "subluxated." This means that certain parts of our spine get out of place.

When this occurs, our bodies cannot function at the fullest capacity. The nervous system that is protected by the spine is unable to do what it is supposed to do and our bodies suffer from pain.

This got me thinking. Often, because we feel pain in our bodies, we resort to medication. We medicate what we think is the issue. We take a pain pill or put a heat pack on a sore spot — hoping for relief. We focus on the perceivable issue and do all we can to medicate the pain instead of addressing the real issue: We have a spine that is out of alignment.

Once we have our spine corrected, often the pain will go away. It may take a while for the pain to leave because our bodies are used to living with it. Another powerful thing called "muscle memory" tends to push our spines back out of alignment. Hence, we need continued adjustment. Yet, if we are consistent with the treatment, we can typically return to full health.

> Living from a place of misalignment will always result in frustration and unanswered prayer

This same principle is also true in our spiritual lives. We have busy lives and many times we suffer from spiritual or emotional trauma. Consequently, we focus on the circumstance or the painful situation that we think is the issue. We medicate the pain in a multitude of ways not realizing that the real issue stems from the fact that we are actually out of alignment with the will of God.

When we come to God, He will bring us into alignment; however, because of our spiritual "muscle memory," quickly we find ourselves out of alignment again. But God is so gracious and always willing to help us. All we have to do is set our eyes on Him and ask for help.

Are you in agreement with His character? Are you in alignment with what He says about Himself and what He says about you? Are you living according to His will? Living from a place of misalignment will always result in frustration and unanswered prayer.

Are you weary of unanswered prayer? Are you weary of feeling like God isn't hearing you? Are you tired of feeling like you are running into a brick wall? Jesus has an answer:

Come to me, all who are weary and heavy-laden, and I will give you rest. Take my yoke upon you and learn from Me, for I am gentle and humble in heart, and you will find rest for your souls. Matthew 11:28,29

Jesus loved to use farming analogies because the culture He was speaking to was an agrarian culture. Although I have never been around an ox, I can still apply the principle to my life. When a new ox was being trained, it was yoked to a mature ox so that it could learn how to operate.

> *A new ox was often trained for plowing or drawing a cart by yoking it with an experienced ox. The yoke kept the young ox from "doing its own thing," and it soon learned obedience to its master. In like manner, we are to commit ourselves to being yoked to Jesus.*[34]

Again, our will is always to be in submission to His will. We are to learn the ways and the paths of God by being yoked to Him. When we align with His will, we become more and more like Him every day.

As we take on the yoke of Jesus and learn from Him, we gain the rest that we have been seeking. Our agreement with His will enables us to operate from a place of rest as we learn how to trust His leadership, no matter what it looks like. We must strive to enter into this rest.[35] We must do all we can to submit ourselves to the correction that is needed to bring us into correct alignment with Jesus.

> **Our agreement with His will enables us to operate from a place of rest as we learn how to trust His leadership**

Then, as a result of our agreement with Him, we become the vessel that God has been looking for. We become the person that is now ready to be used by God for His divine plan. We become the conduit to release the Kingdom of Heaven on earth.

The journey we are seeking begins in the place of faith and truth. When we proclaim God's name, we are being obedient to speak out the nature of God even when it seems fake or we don't feel like it is true. We are aligning ourselves with the truth.

There are many times when reading Scriptures about who God is that I am not sure I believe it. When this happens, I realize that my mind is in opposition to the Word of God, and it needs to be renewed. I become aware of how far out of

---

[34] http://www.awmi.net/bible/mat_11_29
[35] Heb. 4:11

alignment I am with the truth, and I ask the Lord to reveal truth to me as I speak out what He says about Himself.

Sometimes we just have to begin to take a step of faith and speak out in agreement with the truth. Then we allow the Holy Spirit do the work of transforming our minds. Remember, faith is "perceiving as real fact what is not revealed to the senses."[36]

It is interesting that the Bible connects faith and hearing together in the book of Romans:

So then faith comes by hearing, and hearing by the Word of God. Romans 10:17

Something takes place when I begin to hear the truth spoken out loud. Faith begins to take hold where there was no faith before. This is a part of the divine power that is available to us in this battle we are facing. God is actually helping us as we begin to speak out the truth!

Adoration prayer allows us to speak out the truth. As we do, our minds are renewed and our spirits are aligned with the will of God. This leads us to a startling discovery: As we stare into Him, we start to become like Him.

---

[36] Heb. 11:1 AMP

9.

Beholding and becoming

A few years ago I was in Australia on a trip that involved speaking at some local churches. During one of our breaks, our group went to a park to spend time with some young people. As we were sitting there, I noticed an enormous gum tree in the middle of the park. The trunk of the tree was as wide as a car. The size and beauty of this tree were astounding. I also noticed that it was dropping seeds. As I looked at the size of the seed and then looked back at the size of the tree, I was awestruck that the tiny seeds I found were able to produce that enormous tree.

I found it remarkable that those little seeds carry within themselves everything they need to become a tree. The seed does not need to be educated or encouraged. It does not need to spend hours contemplating whether or not it is the plan of God to become a tree. It is a seed that carries the DNA necessary to become a tree.

To turn that seed into a tree, however, is a different story. It must be planted, watered and fertilized. It needs the right atmosphere, the right soil conditions and the right season. Although all those things are certainly vital, it does not take away from the simple fact that the seed carries within itself the ability to become a tree.

This is also true in us:

Grace and peace be multiplied to you in the knowledge of God and of Jesus our Lord; seeing that His divine power has granted to us everything pertaining to life and godliness, through the true knowledge of Him who called us by His own glory and excellence. 2 Peter 1:2-3

Our lives are like that little seed. We have everything we need for life and godliness. Everything we need to become all that we are called to be is already inside of us.

Most of us don't realize, however, that it is in seed form. Although the seed that will produce our future may be present, it needs to be planted, watered and fertilized. It needs the right atmosphere, the right soil conditions and the right season. With care and diligence, the seed that is in us will sprout and bring forth a harvest that will reproduce itself countless times over.

God has planted in us the seed of Christ and is bringing forth in us the image of Jesus

Planting that seed and watering it through prayer represent a great start. Weeding out the doubt and lies we believe about God by declaring God's truth is vital. Understanding that faith is the right atmosphere for growth is essential. What we haven't talked about yet is what kind of plant we are trying to produce.

The seed is not an idea or a concept. It is not a ministry or even our future. The seed *is Christ Himself.* The Holy Spirit planted in us the seed of Christ so that we might bring forth the fruit of Jesus in our lives. The Holy Spirit is not just trying to help us become morally better people. He is laboring to conform us to the image of Christ.[37] His work in us is to reveal Jesus to us and then reveal Jesus through us.

That is why adoration is such a vital thing to do.

To become conformed to the image of Jesus means that we must stare into who He is and get to know Him.

---

[37] Rom. 8:29

We Become What We Behold

Spiritual principles are kind of like laws. Our natural world has laws that we need to understand. For example, the law of gravity is an important one to understand if you plan to jump out of an airplane. There are also spiritual laws that are necessary to understand so that you can walk in all that God has for you. The law of sin and death[38] is the law that keeps you from a relationship with God. The law of life in Christ Jesus sets you free from that law of sin and death. The law of sowing and reaping[39] is a law that can be seen in both the natural and spiritual worlds and can be applied as a natural principle or a spiritual principle.

There is another spiritual principle at work in us as we adore Jesus. What you stare into, you become. If you stare into the issues and circumstances, then you will be overwhelmed by them and will never get victory. But if you stare into the truth of who God is and allow that to determine your life, then you will become like Jesus.

As you agree with the character of God and allow it to be the lens through which you see your life, a transformation begins to take place in you. You are yoking yourself together with Him and learning from Him. You are becoming more and more like Him. You start to think like He thinks. You start to respond like He would respond.

> **As we yoke ourselves together with Him and learn from Him, we become more and more like Him**

As my children grow, I am always amazed by how much they learn just by watching the way I live. I often hear one of my children repeat something that I have said unknowingly. Although they probably do not understand what they are saying, they are imitating what they have seen. It's great when it is something I want them to imitate and horrible when it's something I wish they hadn't seen!

Just as my children are imitators of me, I desire to be somebody that imitates Jesus. I want to stare into Him and learn all I can about who He is so that my life looks more and more like His.

---

[38] Rom. 8:2
[39] Gal. 6:7

David prayed this same prayer in Psalm 27:

One thing I have desired of the Lord, that will I seek: That I may dwell in the house of the Lord all the days of my life, to behold the beauty of the Lord, and to inquire in His temple. Psalm 27:4 NKJV

It was David's desire to remain in the place of staring at the beauty of the Lord. David wasn't trying to escape from life in a melancholy moment. David understood that divine power came from remaining in the place of beholding the beauty of the Lord. For David, this was a lifelong quest to encounter the reality of God. Over and over in the Psalms we see David appealing to the character of God:

I will love You, O Lord, my strength. The Lord is my rock and my fortress and my deliverer; my God, my strength, in whom I will trust; my shield and the horn of my salvation, my stronghold. Psalm 18:1-2

> **David understood that divine power came from remaining in this place of beholding the beauty of the Lord**

The Lord is my shepherd; I shall not want. Psalm 23:1

For the Lord is righteous, He loves righteousness; His countenance beholds the upright. Psalm 11:7

David was not just making up names for God as he went along. Every character attribute was connected to a particular encounter he had with God. David had seen God operate in his life in each of these ways. He had developed a history with God that enabled him to see his life and future with confident hope. David summed up his goal of pursuing the character of God in Psalm 17. This is also our goal and the reason why beholding the Lord is so important:

As for me, I will see your face in righteousness; I shall be satisfied when I awake in your likeness. Psalm 17:15

The goal of all David's searching was to be transformed into the likeness of God! He knew that as he stared into the nature and the character of God, it would bring about a transformation in his own life. The boy who had spent his early years sitting on the side of a hill watching sheep discovered something powerful about God. He found out that God desired to have a relationship with him. The more David pursued this relationship, the more he discovered himself and who he was to become.

You will always become what you stare into. If you stare into your circumstances, your issues, your failures and your mistakes, then you will continue to perpetuate those things. You cannot break the cycle of failure by constantly telling yourself not to fail. You cannot break off the past by living in the past.

To break free of your past failures and have the ability to overcome your circumstances, you need to set your eyes on something that is greater than those things. That is why Paul told the believers to set their minds on things above:

If then you were raised with Christ, seek those things which are above, where Christ is, sitting at the right hand of God. Set your mind on things above, not on things on the earth. For you died, and your life is hidden with Christ in God. When Christ who is our life appears, then you also will appear with Him in glory. Colossians 3:1-4

> **Staring into the character of God and pursuing the knowledge of God are keys that help you break free of the lies**

Staring into the character of God and pursuing the knowledge of God are keys that help you break free of the lies. They help you not only discover God, but discover yourself as well. Then, as you discover your true identity, you gain a new place of authority because *your authority is a by-product of understanding your identity.*

If the son of a wealthy father one day forgets that he is a son, does that mean he loses the legal right to his inheritance? As long as he is a son, he will legally have access to his father's wealth. The only thing that will stand in his way is his own knowledge about who he is. The way he thinks about himself is just as important as the inheritance itself.

What does God say about you?

You are my friends. John 15:14

You are of more value than many sparrows. Matthew 10:31

You are the salt of the earth. Matthew 5:3

Do you not know that you are the temple of God and that the Spirit of God dwells in you? 1 Corinthians 3:16

> **And when you become like Him, you begin to think like Him, act like Him and live out your life like Him**

For you are all sons of God through faith in Christ Jesus. Galatians 3:26

Therefore you are no longer a slave but a son. Galatians 4:7

Now, therefore, you are no longer strangers and foreigners, but fellow citizens with the saints and members of the household of God. Ephesians 2:19

You are all sons of light and sons of the day. 1 Thessalonians 5:5

But you are a chosen generation, a royal priesthood, a holy nation, His own special people, that you may proclaim the praises of Him who called you out of darkness into His marvelous light. 1 Peter 2:9

When you stare into who God is, you will in turn begin to understand who you are. Then, when you know who you are, you will understand the legal rights that you have as a friend, a citizen of Heaven, a chosen generation and a beloved son. When you see His face, you will be transformed to become more like Him. And when you become like Him, you begin to think like Him, act like Him and live out your life like Him.

But we all, with unveiled face, beholding as in a mirror the glory of the Lord, are being transformed into the same image from glory to glory, just as by the Spirit of the Lord. 2 Corinthians 3:18

This is not just a nice thought — this is a promise. As you behold the Lord, you are transformed into His image and conformed to His character. When you know His character, you can better understand His will, because everything God does is an extension of His character.

It's All About His Will

As we discussed in the previous chapter, effective prayer is about His will. It is not about your will, your plans or your ideas; it is about aligning yourself with His will, His plans and His ideas. The more you become like Him, the more you will correctly align yourself with that will and understand its purpose.

Jesus left the earth in the hands of His disciples for a reason. They were to continue the work of both representing and demonstrating the Kingdom of God. They knew the character and the will of God because they had seen it demonstrated through the life of Jesus.

Now, as co-laborers with Him, they were to continue to demonstrate the Kingdom they had experienced. In dynamic partnership with the Holy Spirit, they were to represent the Kingdom and in doing so make disciples throughout the nations of the world.

We also have an invitation into the same dynamic partnership. God is inviting us to co-labor with Him by releasing His name and character in the earth. God is not just looking for workers; He is looking for partnership.

> **We have a divine invitation and responsibility to hear His heart and then be those who pray in agreement with His character and His will**

We have a divine invitation and responsibility to hear His heart and then be those who pray in agreement with His character and His will. As we do this, we become the vehicles through which Heaven touches earth.

The day that I first began to understand this concept was life-changing. In a moment, my prayer life changed. I was no longer trying to convince God to do things for me. I was no longer wondering what to pray for. I began to pray over the character attributes that I had learned in the place of adoration and I realized that these same prayers had power on them to shift the circumstances that I faced.

I realized that God had given us His character as the launching point for a counterattack on the enemy. If it didn't agree with God's will and His character, I had a target. I wasn't just praying for the things that I needed; I was looking for the things that didn't line up with who God was and what His Kingdom represented. Then I realized that this is exactly what He told us to do:

But seek first His Kingdom and His righteousness, and all these things will be added to you. Matthew 6:33

I discovered that God is looking for those who will seek His Kingdom first. Out of this "Kingdom first" mentality, God would grant them the answers they were seeking. It might not look like what they initially expected, but it would be in agreement with His character, and that was all that really mattered.

I already knew what the Kingdom looked like because I had been staring into the character of the King. As I adored the Lord for who He was, I began to realize that He was offering us a gift in His character. You and I, as sons and daughters of the King, could take the authority that was available through the revealed character of God and apply it to the circumstances that we faced.

As a result, we become the people who God uses to release the Kingdom of Heaven.

Before you read these next few chapters, make sure you watch the fifth and last video: "Proclamation Prayer." You can watch the video by going to **www.benwoodward.com/truthstudy5**, *entering the password "truth" and following the prompts.*

10.

The Word of God is like a hammer

In the book of Isaiah, God declares some fascinating truths about His Word. When we grasp the enormous consequences of what He is saying, our prayers will no longer just be a simple exercise in spirituality. When we understand the power of the Word of God, we will find a weapon that cannot fail:

For my thoughts are not your thoughts, nor are your ways my ways," declares the Lord. "For as the heavens are higher than the earth, so are my ways higher than your ways and my thoughts than your thoughts. For as the rain and the snow come down from Heaven, and do not return there without watering the earth and making it bear and sprout, and furnishing seed to the sower and bread to the eater, so will my Word be which goes forth from my mouth; It will not return to me empty, without accomplishing what I desire, and without succeeding in the matter for which I sent it. Isaiah 55:8-11

God's Word is already at work in the earth, and it will never fail. He will accomplish all that He said He would. That is the promise we can stand on when we begin to declare God's Word over our own lives.

When we begin to speak out the words that God has already spoken before, we enter into an agreement that God has with His Word. That agreement states that His Word will not return empty without accomplishing all that He sent it out to do. When we open up our mouths and, with hearts full of faith, begin to speak out the truth of who He is, the earth will have no option but to fall in line with the Kingdom of God.

In faith, we can open our mouths and declare His nature with confidence, no matter what the natural circumstance says. Why? Because the same "Word" lives in us.

Paul describes it this way:

But if the Spirit of Him who raised Jesus from the dead dwells in you, He who raised Christ from the dead will also give life to your mortal bodies through His Spirit who dwells in you. Romans 8:11

> **There is no power in your natural flesh, but there is power in the "word of God" that will not return void**

The same Spirit who took the dead Jesus and raised Him to life is dwelling inside of you. This same Spirit will also give life to your body and empower you in the same way. It is this Spirit who empowers your words to be more than just simple words. There is no power in your natural flesh, but there is power in the "Word of God" that dwells in you.

Encountering The God That Heals

I had a powerful experience related to this in my own life a few years ago.

I married the most amazing woman in 2004. When we first got married, we made a decision that we were going to let the Lord give us children in the timing He wanted to. We would trust Him to know the perfect time for that to come to pass for our family.

One day, after a few years of not being able to get pregnant, my wife was admitted to the emergency room due to an immense amount of pain in her abdomen. We found out that she had a cyst on her left ovary that was the size of a baby's head. She needed immediate surgery and during the course of our visits with the doctor and physician, we discovered that my wife was suffering from the effects of severe endometriosis.

Endometriosis is a crippling reproductive disease that affects many women. In its mild form it causes pain and scarring internally. In its severe form it can lead to infertility. This was not good news.

After the surgery, the doctor told us that our chances of getting pregnant were slim and that we needed to try to get pregnant as soon as possible. Realizing that my wife was suffering from endometriosis answered a lot of questions as to why her health had been under attack. We began to pray for an answer.

Another two years passed and my wife was still unable to get pregnant. This was very upsetting for her as month after month she expected to take a positive pregnancy test and it turned out negative. I knew the promises the Lord had given to both of us about our family so, despite the circumstances, I remained confident. This was just another obstacle that stood in the way of what God had planned for our lives, but it did not lessen the frustration.

We needed a miracle.

During this time, I was asked to lead worship for a local conference held in Kansas City. At the conference, a man named Masahida Kanayama was sharing about the work he was doing in New York. Dr. Kanayama just happened to be one of the top endometriosis doctors in the U.S. He has a success rate that is exponentially greater than any other doctor in his field. In a dream, the Lord revealed to him a new medical device that he was using to see thousands of women set free from the curse of endometriosis.

I approached him after one of the sessions and began to tell him about my wife. I asked him if he could pray for her. He was glad to do that and after praying, we exchanged phone numbers.

Three days later, I received a phone call from him. He told me that the Lord had given him a vision of where the disease was in my wife's body and that we needed to come and have surgery immediately. He was confident the Lord would heal her and "very soon we would be able to have children."

Both my wife and I were overwhelmed because we knew this was an answer to both of our prayers. Subsequently, we began to plan our trip to New York for my wife to undergo surgery with Dr. Kanayama.

But this was not going to be as easy as we had initially thought. About a month before the surgery was scheduled, I received a phone call from the office manager at Dr. Kanayama's office. She called to inform me that we needed a $7,000 deposit before they were able to continue with preparations for the surgery.

At that time, my wife and I were working for a prayer ministry. Our income was primarily from monthly supporters and it was not a lot. We were blessed if we had two pennies to rub together let alone any savings that amounted to thousands of dollars. I knew that we were unable to come up with money ourselves but I was still confident that this was the answer that the Lord had provided for us.

> We laughed because God is always good, because the devil is a liar and because the circumstance had to change because of who our God is!

A friend once told me, "When the circumstances become too great to handle, push the furniture out of the room and throw a party." My wife and I did just that. We pushed the furniture back in our living room, we got down on the floor and we declared the goodness of God over our lives! We stayed on the floor and laughed about our situation.

We laughed because God is always good, because the devil is a liar and because the circumstance had to change because of who our God is! This mountain — this financial obstacle — could not stand in opposition to my Father who is the God of the impossible! He had promised us a family who would love Him well, and this circumstance was a small thing for our God.

That night, a friend came over and prayed with us. He felt the Lord tell him that we would receive double the amount of money we needed and my wife would be healed. We took that promise and stood on it. I was confident that the God who enabled Sarah to give birth in her old age, kept the children of Israel from sickness in the desert, spoke to Moses, sent fire from Heaven for Elijah, rescued David from Goliath's hand and healed Naaman the leper was the same God who would answer us.

The week after this took place, I was leading worship for another conference. The leader of the conference asked me to tell a group of about one hundred people about the circumstances that we were facing. He asked the attendees that if they felt led to give, they could find us at the end of the service. Over the next two days, we miraculously raised double the amount of money that we needed! To this day I am so grateful to those few who loved us so well in our time of need.

Because of the money we received, we were able to go to New York for the surgery. We met Dr. Kanayama at his office and after a few tests my wife was booked in for surgery. What should have been a one-and-a-half-hour surgery ended up being a four-hour surgery. During the surgery, Dr. Kanayama saw that one of my wife's ovaries had been 90% destroyed by the disease. Instead of just removing the ovary like most doctors would, he began to declare "the God who heals" over the ovary. He spoke to that ovary and as he spoke the ovary began to regrow. By the end of the surgery the ovary was completely restored!

When I met with Dr. Kanayama after the surgery, he looked at me and said, "In six weeks, your wife will be pregnant." Six weeks later my wife was pregnant. Five years later we have three amazing children.

God's Word Is Like A Hammer

I believe that the release of this miracle was the result of how we responded to the obstacle that we were faced with. By pushing the furniture out of the living room, getting on the floor and declaring our trust in the God of the impossible, we were able to get into faith and not into fear.

> When we speak out the word of God, we enter into agreement with His Kingdom

When we laughed at the problems, we came into agreement with God's Word and His Word in us became like a hammer that shattered the obstacles in our way.

Jeremiah 23.29 says this about the Word of God:

Is not my word like a fire?" says the Lord, "and like a hammer that breaks the rock in pieces?

When we speak out the Word of God, we enter into agreement with His Kingdom. His Word through us becomes like a hammer that breaks the rocks in pieces. It becomes the necessary tool needed to remove the obstacles in our path.

Sometimes, the obstacles are set there by God Himself so that we will take up the authority given to us to speak to the mountain. At other times, the enemy puts a stumbling block in our way so that we will become discouraged and give up. The answer is the same no matter what we are faced with. We open up our mouth and declare who God is by speaking out the Word of God. When we do this, we begin to tear down the strongholds that exist due to the lies we have believed about who God is.

The Word of God, when it is paired with faith and spoken out of the mouth of a son or daughter of God, has the power to bring God's Kingdom to any situation. The power does not come because of a magic formula. It is the result of the Holy Spirit who works through us.

This partnership between Heaven and earth is a reality. Many believers in the church have been content with far less because they didn't know it was available to them. I am excited for the day when hundreds and thousands of believers across the earth realize the power that is available to them. I live in expectation for the day when they become the conduits for the Kingdom of Heaven they were always meant to be.

11.

The power of proclamation

Speaking out in agreement with the Word of God and seeing the miraculous happen as a result are not new ideas. Scripture shows us many examples of men and women who declared something and it happened just as they spoke. Elijah operated with the same power when he prayed, and the earth stopped giving rain for three and a half years.[40] Moses was told to speak to the rock to bring forth water.[41] The children of Israel shouted and the walls of Jericho came down.[42] These are supernatural occurrences that took place in the lives of people who had faith.

When Jesus was faced with an obstacle, He responded in the same way:

And there arose a fierce gale of wind, and the waves were breaking over the boat so much that the boat was already filling up. Jesus Himself was in the stern, asleep on the cushion; and they woke Him and said to Him, "Teacher, do you not care that we are perishing?" And He got up and rebuked the wind and said to the sea, "Hush, be still." And the wind died down and it became perfectly calm. And He said to them, "Why are you afraid? Do you still have no faith?" They became very much afraid and said to one another, "Who then is this, that even

---

[40] James 5:17
[41] Numbers 20:8
[42] Joshua 6

the wind and the sea obey Him?" Mark 4:37-41

Jesus' response to a life-threatening situation was not just to pray and ask the Father to do something, but to speak to the situation itself. The sea was threatening to overwhelm the boat and was causing the disciples serious distress! Jesus stood up, spoke to the sea and it obeyed Him. And then He continued by rebuking the disciples for a lack of faith!

Jesus' authority extended even to natural elements and that same authority has been given to us if we walk in the knowledge of God and in faith. Jesus told His disciples on more than one occasion to speak to the issue itself and it would obey them:

> **There is a forgotten power in our words that needs to be remembered, but it must be restored in partnership with the knowledge of God**

Truly I say to you, whoever says to this mountain, "Be taken up and cast into the sea," and does not doubt in his heart, but believes that what he says is going to happen, it will be granted him. Mark 11:23

Jesus did not tell them to ask the Father to do something, but to speak to the mountain itself. Other versions say that the mountain itself would obey them because they spoke to it in faith. This is a remarkable promise for us as well.

The Power Of Our Words

There is a forgotten power in our words that needs to be remembered, but it must be restored in partnership with the knowledge of God. This is one of the greatest weapons we have in this war:

Death and life are in the power of the tongue, and those who love it will eat its fruit. Proverbs 18:21

The mystery of why God would put that much power into our words astounds me. This is not merely a metaphorical idea that we apply when we are trying to convince our children to treat each other with respect. The power to bring forth the Kingdom of Heaven has been given to the sons of men, and one of the methods is through what comes out of their mouths.

I used to believe that this verse was primarily related to my own internal life in God. But then I began to see how the words I speak also have great power to bring life or death over the people around me as well. There is not a single person I know who is not impacted when someone speaks words of life over them. I have seen many lives transformed by a few simple words of encouragement, just as I have seen lives destroyed by a careless remark.

The Apostle James had a lot to say about what comes out of our mouths. He considered the tongue such a powerful weapon that he said if you could control it, you would be able to control your whole body!

For we all stumble in many things. If anyone does not stumble in word, he is a perfect man, able also to bridle the whole body. Now if we put the bits into the horses' mouths so that they will obey us, we direct their entire body as well. Look at the ships also, though they are so great and are driven by strong winds, are still directed by a very small rudder wherever the inclination of the pilot desires. So also the tongue is a small part of the body, and yet it boasts of great things. James 3:2-5

James tells us that the tongue is like a rudder. To bring our mind and spirit into alignment with the truth, we need to use our mouth. Just as a horse is pointed in the right direction through the use of a bit in its mouth, so we can point our minds in a new direction by what we speak out of our mouths. In the same way that a very small rudder directs a ship, we can be directed by the way that we speak.

> To bring our minds and spirit into alignment with the truth, we need to use our mouth

As we discovered in the last chapter, if you take the Word of God, apply faith and then speak it out, things change. Add that to the "fervent effectual prayer of a righteous man," and you have an unstoppable weapon against the work of the enemy.

Proclamation Prayer

The kind of prayer I am talking about is what I call "proclamation prayer." Proclamation prayer is active and forceful.

Our words are powerful. What we speak out is powerful. Even people who don't believe in Jesus understand how powerful our words are. According to bestselling author and international consultant Rebecca L. Morgan:

"We have opportunities every day to use our words to cut or to heal. Every time we open our mouth, we have a choice. You and I have the power to make others feel great — or horrible. With that power comes responsibility. We have the obligation to use that power in the best way possible for our fellow humans.

In my life's journey I'm learning to be vigilant in my awareness and sensitivity to not only the effect others' words have on me, but on the long-lasting effect my words have on others. It's true, 'Words not only affect us temporarily — they change us.'"[43]

The world is aware that words can bring about great emotional change. We, however, have a far greater responsibility because our words bring about far greater change. As Christians, our words have transformative power because of the Spirit of Christ in us.

> **Proclamation prayer is taking the character of God and declaring it over your life and circumstance**

This will make you stop and think about the careless words you say! Your words have the power to release destiny. Your words have the power to bring change when they agree with the "Word of God" that dwells in you.

God is working to see His will established in the earth, and He looks for those who desire to live in agreement with Him. They become the conduit that Heaven works through. One of the most powerful ways this happens is by simply proclaiming His nature. Proclamation prayer is taking the character of God and declaring it over your life and circumstance. It is agreeing with the things that God says about Himself. Because God's will is an extension of His character, you are also aligning with His will.

When you do this, things begin to change.

Using what God has already told you about Himself, you can now focus your prayer on the issue in front of you. Speak to the circumstance about who God is. This allows His name to be magnified and glorified in your life. Through proclamation prayer, you begin to digest the Word of God and it moves from

---

[43] http://www.rebeccamorgan.com/articles/mgmt/mgmt2.html - Rebecca L. Morgan, CSP, CMC

your head into your heart. To produce transformation, however, you must begin to speak it out and use the weapon that God gave you — your voice. His word, when it is spoken out of your mouth, has the power to silence the enemy and release the Kingdom of God.

Confidence In The Name Of The Lord

As you being to proclaim God's nature over your circumstances, faith begins to arise. You become courageous. You become bold. You start to think things that before seemed out of reach. Israel's King David experienced this same transformation, and it enabled him to have unshakable faith — even when he was faced with a giant.

Then David said to the Philistine, "You come to me with a sword and with a spear and with a javelin, but I come to you in the name of the Lord of hosts, the God of the armies of Israel, whom you have defied. 1 Samuel 17:45

David's confidence was not in his own ability. His confidence was in the name of the Lord. David's strength came from knowing God and believing who He was toward him. David had already cultivated the knowledge of God as a shepherd while tending sheep and now he was empowered to be a giant killer. This same giant-killing fearlessness is available to you as you proclaim the nature and character of God over your life and circumstances.

When you are in agreement with His will, His Kingdom is released through you

When you proclaim the character of God in the face of difficulty, the power of God is activated in your life. Knowing the character of God allows you to live in agreement with His will. When you are in agreement with His will, His Kingdom is released through you. As you begin to proclaim the nature of God, the natural world begins to respond. Your circumstances begin to change. Your future begins to look different. Your whole life begins to be aligned with the purpose of God. Proclamation activates the power of God in the midst of circumstances because you are aligning your heart with God's will by declaring His nature. When you open your mouth, you become a conduit between Heaven and earth. You are given the opportunity to affect the natural realm by proclaiming the nature of God!

This idea of proclaiming God's character over your life is more than just a cute idea. It is the reality that you need in order to overcome the obstacles you will face. We have all spent too much time cultivating the language of fear and doubt. In response to this, we need to spend just as much time speaking out truth and cultivating a language of faith and confidence.

Proclamation enables you to be in agreement with God's character and causes your life to be in agreement with His will. God's Word is already at work in the earth; however, when it finds an earthly vessel that it can work through, a divine partnership takes place, and we get to join in the story. That is the power of proclamation.

12.

The answer to your unanswered prayer

We are at war. This war is relentless and will require much from us if we are to overcome and be who God called us to be. But we have divinely powerful weapons at our disposal. If we cultivate a life of adoration and proclamation prayer, we can change the course of this war.

But we live in a culture that loves the microwaveable, quick fix, easy does it solution. We do everything we can to make life as easy and painless as possible. But it hasn't been working. Our joy is far too quickly taken from us. Our hope is dashed all to easily. Something has to change, because what we have been doing up to this point has failed us.

I believe that it's time we took a stand against the apathy that has allowed the lies of the enemy to sow doubt into our lives. It's time that we woke up and realized that we are at war.

The Church That Fell Asleep

In the book of Revelation, John relays some pretty intense words that Jesus had for some local churches at the time. One particular church was located in the region of Sardis.

This city had an interesting history. Twice, it was overrun by its enemies because of simple neglect:

> The previous history of Sardis should have warned them concerning the possibility of sudden and unexpected judgment. Although the situation of the city was ideal for defense, as it stood high above the valley of Hermus and was surrounded by deep cliffs almost impossible to scale, Sardis had twice before fallen because of overconfidence and failure to watch. In 549 B.C. the Persian King Cyrus had ended the rule of Croesus by scaling the cliffs under the cover of darkness. In 214 B.C. the armies of Antiochus the Great (III) captured the city by the same method.[44]

This great city was not lacking in men or equipment. It was not lacking in natural defense. What it lacked was the vigilance of those who were supposed to be guarding it. With this in mind, let's look at what Jesus says to the Church in Sardis:

> And to the angel of the church in Sardis write: The words of him who has the seven spirits of God and the seven stars. "I know your works. You have the reputation of being alive, but you are dead. Wake up, and strengthen what remains and is about to die, for I have not found your works complete in the sight of my God. Remember, then, what you received and heard."
> Revelation 3:1-3 ESV

You shall know the truth and the truth will set you free

If you are at war, then you must live like someone who is at war. A soldier on the front lines does not focus on how to get comfortable. He has one goal — to finish the task before him and return safely to the people he loves. He does whatever is necessary so that the war may be won. There is a determination that exists because he understands both the circumstances and the urgency of the situation he lives in.

Jesus brought a stunning rebuke to the church of Sardis. They had become complacent in the war and had lost their way. They had a reputation of being alive but it was a false representation of what was going on. Jesus implored them to go back and "remember." Go back and remember the truth and what they had received. It is such a simple and elegant solution. It is the same solution for you. You already have the answer. You shall know the truth and

---

[44] http://www.walvoord.com/article/261

the truth will set you free.

Our conflict is a battle over the truth. Is God who He says He is? Can He be trusted? Every day we are faced with those lies and every day we must respond by declaring the truth. Every day we have to open up our mouths and come into agreement with the Word of God. When we become complacent, we allow the enemy to creep over the walls of our city and bring destruction.

But as we adore Him and fall in love with Him, we are transformed into His likeness. As we proclaim His nature, our perspective changes and the Kingdom of Heaven is released. What will it take for us to believe that God has empowered us to be overcomers? What will it take for us to realize that the power we have been looking for from an external source has been inside of us the whole time? It is Christ in us, the hope of glory!

When we pray in agreement with that "hope," we are empowered to become the answer we are looking for. We become a partner in releasing the Kingdom of Heaven on the earth.

The war we are in is a war of attrition. It is designed to wear us down so that we become so weary of life that we fall asleep on the watch. The enemy wants us to stop giving thanks and to stop rejoicing in the goodness of God. He wants to convince us that God is not who He says He is so that we will cut the lines of communication and give up.

I have good news, though. We are not trying to scale an impossible mountain. We are talking about entering into the fullness of a relationship that we were always designed to have. This is about knowing the *"love that surpasses knowledge—that you may be filled to the measure of all the fullness of God."*[45] The Kingdom of God is a Kingdom of relationship. It is divine partnership that He is seeking. He wants to give us the right tools and the right weapons so that we can be those who have overcome the enemy.

It is time that we became a people of hope. We can only do that when we know who God is and who we are to Him. But there is a battle that rages around us to deny us that knowledge. We need weapons to defeat the lies. We need the right tools to flourish in this day and age. Thankfully, we have been given divine weapons that tear down the lies. All that is required of us is to renew our minds and align them with the truth. The most powerful way to do

---
[45] Eph. 3:19

that is to take the truth we know about God and pray it back to Him. Through adoration and proclamation we can renew our minds, cultivate faith and see a radical change take place in our lives.

The truth will set us free.

How to Pray Adoration and Proclamation Prayers.

Find out what God says about Himself.

The first step requires us to go on a journey of discovery. The easiest way I have found to do this is to ask myself, "What is the biggest obstacle I am facing at this point in time?" Then I go to the Bible and find out what God says about that issue. What does He say about Himself related to that issue? If I am faced with the issue of uncertainty regarding the future, then I will search the Scripture for others that faced the same uncertainty. How did Jacob survive the uncertainty in his life when his brother was trying to kill him? Scripture says that Jacob discovered God as a shepherd. So in answer to Jacob's question, God revealed himself as a shepherd who cares for His people, just like a shepherd cares for his flock.

Continue by discovering all the other places in Scripture where that attribute is revealed.

In the example we just used, I would then go and find as many places as I could that speak about God or Jesus as a shepherd. David speaks of God as a shepherd in Psalm 23. Jesus spoke often of Himself as the Good Shepherd. Write down all the times that this attribute is revealed in Scripture because this will be the dynamite that you need to break down the walls of doubt that have been built up over years. Not only will you be creating a catalogue of the attributes of God, but you will also fall increasingly in love with the Bible as a result, because you will see it as a tool to discover Jesus!

Begin to speak to God about who He is.

This does not have to be an earth-shattering event. Prayer is simply communication, so let your prayer be simple and real. Do not attempt to set a world record for the amount of time spent in prayer. Begin with what you are able to and read through the scriptures you have written down about the attribute of God you are focused on. When I pray adoration or proclamation prayers, I focus on three things:

1. What does the Bible say about this attribute of God?
2. Where have I seen this attribute in my own life?
3. Where has God shown Himself like this in history?

As I pray, I use these three things to form the basis of my prayers. Beginning with the scripture and attribute, I begin to tell Him who He is.

Write down the things God is speaking to you as you pray.

Often as you are speaking to God about who He is, God will begin to give you a greater level of understanding about the very thing you are praying. It is just like the angels in Heaven who cry, "Holy, Holy, Holy!" Every time they look at the Father they are given a greater revelation of the holiness of God and it increases over time. As you develop new language and give more time to the place of prayer, God will respond by unlocking a new understanding about Himself.

Always end with thankfulness and a new perspective!

As we discover who God is, we will discover who we are. This should lead to thankfulness! Being thankful will keep us out of the bitterness that comes because of delayed answers. Sometimes, we do not get immediate answers. But as we discover who He is, we can trust Him because we know He is good. When delay occurs, the answer is to step it up and increase your thankfulness! Thankfulness gives us correct perspective, which will enable us to maintain a spirit of expectancy and faith.

Alphabetical Attributes Of God

(For a more in-depth version, check out the Adoration and Proclamation Prayer Book available at www.benwoodward.com)

A

The Available God

God is our refuge and strength, a very present (available) help in trouble. Psalm 46:1

The Approachable God

But Jesus said, "Let the children alone, and do not hinder them from coming to me; for the kingdom of heaven belongs to such as these." Matthew 19:14

B

The Better Than God

For a day in your courts is better than a thousand outside. I would rather stand at the threshold of the house of my God than dwell in the tents of wickedness. Psalm 84:10

The Burden Bearing God

Cast your burden upon the Lord and He will sustain you; He will never allow the righteous to be shaken. Psalm 55:22

C

The Comforter

I will ask the Father, and He will give you another Helper (Comforter), that He may be with you forever. John 14:16

The Compassionate God

I Myself will make all My goodness pass before you, and will proclaim the name of the Lord before you; and I will be gracious to whom I will be gracious, and will show compassion on whom I will show compassion. Exodus 33:19

D

The Determined God

For God so loved the world that He gave His only begotten Son, that whoever believes in Him shall not perish, but have eternal life. John 3:16

The Delivering God

My lovingkindness and my fortress, my stronghold and my deliverer, my shield and He in whom I take refuge, who subdues my people under me. Psalm 144:2

E

The Eternal God

"I am the Alpha and the Omega," says the Lord God, "who is and who was and who is to come, the Almighty." Revelation 1:8

The Excellent God

Having become as much better than the angels, as He has inherited a more excellent name than they. Hebrews 1:4

F

The God Who is For Me

What then shall we say to these things? If God is for us, who is against us... Christ Jesus is who died, yes, rather who was raised, who is at the right hand of God, who also intercedes for us. Rom. 8:31,34

The Forgiving God

If we confess our sins, He is faithful and righteous to forgive us our sins and to cleanse us from all unrighteousness. 1 John 1:9

G

The Generous God

Every good thing given and every perfect gift is from above, coming down from the Father of lights, with whom there is no variation or shifting shadow. James 1:17

The Good God

Beloved, do not imitate what is evil, but what is good. The one who does good is of God; the one who does evil has not seen God. 3 John 1:11

The Glorious God

Now therefore, our God, we thank You, and praise Your glorious name. 1 Chr. 29.13

H

The Happy God

You have loved righteousness and hated lawlessness; Therefore God, Your God, has anointed You with the oil of gladness more than Your companions. Hebrews 1:9

The God Who Heals

Jesus was going through all the cities and villages, teaching in their synagogues and proclaiming the gospel of the kingdom, and healing every kind of disease and every kind of sickness. Matthew 9:35

I

The Innocent God

God made Him who had no sin to be sin for us, so that in Him we might become the righteousness of God. 2 Corinthians 5:21

The Intercessory God

Therefore He is able also to save forever those who draw near to God through Him, since He always lives to make intercession for them. Hebrews 7:25

J

The Just God

Rejoice greatly, O daughter of Zion! Shout in triumph, O daughter of Jerusalem! Behold, your king is coming to you; He is just and endowed with salvation, humble, and mounted on a donkey, even on a colt, the foal of a donkey. Zechariah 9:9

The Joyful God

And He brought forth His people with joy, His chosen ones with a joyful shout. Psalm 105:43

K

The Kind God

Be kind to one another, tender-hearted, forgiving each other, just as God in Christ also has forgiven you. Ephesians 4:32

The Keeper God

The Lord is your keeper; The Lord is your shade on your right hand. ...The Lord will protect you from all evil; He will keep your soul. Psalm 121:5,7

L

The Loving God

The Lord appeared to him from afar, saying, "I have loved you with an everlasting love; therefore I have drawn you with lovingkindness." Jeremiah 31:3

God The Light

Though I dwell in darkness, the Lord is a light for me. Micah 7:8

M

The Majestic God

Who is like You among the gods, O Lord? Who is like You, majestic in holiness, awesome in praises, working wonders? Ex. 15:11

The God Of Miracles

God was performing extraordinary miracles by the hands of Paul. Acts 19:11

N

The Near God

Draw near to God and He will draw near to you. James 4:8

The Nothing Is Impossible God

For nothing will be impossible with God. Luke 1:37

O

The Overcoming God

These things I have spoken to you, so that in me you may have peace. In the world you have tribulation, but take courage; I have overcome the world. John 16:33

The Outstanding God

My beloved is dazzling and ruddy, outstanding among ten thousand. Song 5:10

P

God The Perfecter

Fixing our eyes on Jesus, the author and perfecter of faith, who for the joy set before Him endured the cross, despising the shame, and has sat down at the right hand of the throne of God. Hebrews 12:2

The Protector God

The LORD will protect him and keep him alive, and he shall be called blessed upon the earth; and do not give him over to the desire of his enemies. Psalm 41:2

R

God The Rock

The Rock! His work is perfect, for all His ways are just. Deuteronomy 32:4

The Restoring God

He restores my soul; He guides me in the paths of righteousness for His name's sake. Psalm 23:3

S

The Savior God

I, even I, am the LORD, and there is no savior besides Me. Isaiah 43:11

The Satisfying God

Who satisfies your years with good things, so that your youth is renewed like the eagle. Psalm 103:5

T

The Triumphant God

When He had disarmed the rulers and authorities, He made a public display of them, having triumphed over them through Him. Colossians 2:15

The God Who Is Truth

It is the Spirit who testifies, because the Spirit is the truth. 1 John 5:6

U

The Upright God

A God of faithfulness and without injustice, Righteous and upright is He. Deuteronomy 32:4

The Unchanging God

For I, the LORD, do not change; therefore you, O sons of Jacob, are not consumed. Malachi 3:6

V

The Victorious God

The LORD your God is in your midst, a victorious warrior. Zephaniah 3:17

The God Who Has A Voice

The LORD also thundered in the heavens, and the Most High uttered His voice. Psalm 18:13

W

The Winning God

I am the first and the last, and the living One; and I was dead, and behold, I am alive forevermore, and I have the keys of death and of Hades. Revelation 1:17-18

Proclamation Prayer Example

(For more proclamation prayers, check out the Adoration and Proclamation Prayer Book available at www.benwoodward.com)

The God Who Is For Me

Father, I run to You today as I come to discover the truth about the "God who is for me." When I think about my life, I realize that most of it has been spent running from You rather than running to You. I realize that I have not seen You as a God who is concerned about my needs or my heart. I have only ever seen You as a God who is waiting for me to make a mistake so that You can punish me. I have spent most of my life trying to give You as little time as possible because I thought You were not happy about being with me. Today, all that changes. I come to proclaim Your nature as the God who is passionately for me.

You Are 'For Me' With Compassion

Father, today, I declare the very words that Jesus spoke when He was describing the kind of God You are. He said in His story about the prodigal son, "But when he was yet a great way off, his father saw him, and had compassion, and ran, and fell on his neck, and kissed him."[46] Lord, Your heart is so full of compassion toward me. Even when I am a great way off, You have those eyes that burn with a flame of fire for me. You see me even at my weakest point and still You say about me that I "have ravished [Your]

---

[46] Luke 15:20

heart with one glance of [my] eye."⁴⁷ Who would run into the arms of a son who had wasted the family fortune? You are so completely for me that You will overlook my failures to reach me and let me know how much You love me. Father, I declare today that You are the God who is for me in such a way that You will run to meet me. I know that I have pictured You as stoic and unemotional, but You are far from that. You may sit in the heavens as King of Kings but You are also the Father who runs to meet His sons and daughters in need. You have such a plan for me, and You are so full of compassion, even when I fail to walk in the path You have placed before me. You love me and are for me, even still today.

You Have A Plan For Me

I declare what You said through the prophet Jeremiah, "For I know the plans that I have for you,' declares the LORD, 'plans for welfare and not for calamity to give you a future and a hope."⁴⁸ Father, I know that these were not just idle words spoken years ago to another generation. You have a great plan for my future, and even now You are working to see it accomplished. Your plan cannot fail when it comes to me because You are the God who has never failed in anything You have set out to do. When I commit my ways to the Lord, there is not a thing that could stand in the way of Your will and Your plan for my life being fulfilled. I know at times it seems like things may have been delayed, but I will yet declare that You are the God who is for me. You are fully aware of the plans You have for me and I am confident that not one thing has been forgotten. You will accomplish what You said You would by giving me a future and a hope. Thank You that You are restoring hope to me today, by reminding me that You have not forgotten me. You have not forgotten any of the promises You made to me concerning my life. Every time I feel myself getting into despair, I just remember your name. When I remember Your word, I am set ablaze again to declare that You are the God who is for me. You have a plan for me. You have a future for me. You have a desire that I would live all my days grounded in hope because of who You are. I remember all the things that You have done in the past for me. The way You have loved me, the way You have provided for me and the way You have planted my feet on the Rock that is Your son Jesus. I will not let my circumstances dictate my belief about how You feel about me; I will let Your word remind me that You are for me.

You Are My Success

Father, I declare the words that Jesus spoke in the book of Matthew: "And who of you by being worried can add a single hour to his life?"⁴⁹ How much time and energy have I wasted by not seeing You as the God who is for me? I have worried about my life far too much. Today, I make my declaration that I will no longer live a life of worry. I will

---

⁴⁷ Song 4:9 NKJV
⁴⁸ Jer. 29:11
⁴⁹ Matt. 6:27

live a life that proves I am trusting in the God who is for me. I proclaim that all that I am is Yours, so I give You permission to do with me as You see best. You know exactly how I was made and You know exactly what I need to fulfill my purpose in this life. I declare that because You are the God who is for me, I cannot fail in what I am called to do. I have only one option, and that is to succeed. I want to see my life differently today; I want to see it through the eyes of the God who is for my success. I know that this does not always mean an easy or comfortable life, but it does mean that I can trust it will be the best life possible. I am confident that no matter what happens, You are working behind the scenes to ensure my success.

You Delight In Me

I proclaim today the same words that King David wrote in the Psalms when he was delivered from his enemies: "[You] brought me forth also into a broad place; [You] rescued me, because [You] delighted in me."[50] Father, I declare that You are the God who takes me from a narrow, poor understanding of who You are to a broad place where I can fully understand who You are. I confess that my understanding of You has been limited by my experience in this life. But You are not limited by my lack of understanding! You know my weak frame and that is why You are so determined to rescue me and set me in a broad place. You are on a mission to radically transform the way I think about You. Once You have done that, You will enable me to see myself rightly through Your eyes. Father, what an incredible thing it is to know that You delight in me. I know that this delight does not come from what I do for You but who I am to You. You are the God who is for me and delights in me today and all the days of my life. You may be sad over my sin at times, but You always delight in me as a child.

You Came To Save Me

Father, I declare that the greatest thing You did to prove how much You are for me was to send Your son, Jesus. I declare what Jesus said in the book of John: "[You] so loved the world, that [You] gave [Your] only begotten Son, that whoever believes in Him shall not perish, but have eternal life. For [You] did not send the Son into the world to judge the world, but that the world might be saved through Him."[51] Father, I know that so many times I have heard this verse and overlooked the power of what it means to me. But today I stare into the truth that is Your word and declare that You love me. Your love was so great that You ransacked heaven on my behalf and sent Your Son to save me. You said that You did not come to condemn us but to save us. So Father, I proclaim today that You are for me, far more than I could have ever dreamed was possible. You proved it by sending Your very own son into the world to ensure that not only am I saved eternally, but I am also given the chance to enter into the perfect will

---

[50] Psa. 18:19
[51] John 3:16-17

of God for my life today. Father, I believe in Your son. I believe that You are for me and I believe that You have loved me with an everlasting love. I declare what Jesus also said in the book of John, "that [I] may be perfected in unity, so that the world may know that You sent [Jesus], and loved [me], even as You have loved [Jesus]."[52] Father, I proclaim that You love me with the same measure that You love Jesus! How could I ever doubt that You are for me? How can I ever again doubt whether or not You have my future in the palm of Your hands? Jesus never once doubted whether or not You were for Him and just as You were for Jesus, so You are for me.

Father, I will not doubt You any longer, I will believe that You are for me no matter what the circumstances say. No matter what happens in the earth, in my life, or in my family, I know that You are the God who is for me. Today, I stand upon the truth that God is for me.

---

[52] John 17:23

Adoration Exercise

Simple Adoration Introduction (30 minute exercise)

Part 1.

1. Take an attribute of God in the "A" section and read the verse related to it.
2. Say this phrase - "Thank you that you are [attribute] to me." That's it! Don't say anything else. Don't ask for anything, just say the phrase above.
3. Repeat the above steps with attributes from "B" through "G."

Part 2.

1. Using the same attributes you just used in step 1, think about how God has displayed himself to you in that way.
2. Pray using the same attributes: "Thank you that you are [attribute] to me. I remember how you showed me this part of your character [use whatever circumstance you have thought about]."

Part 3.

1. Look through the list of attributes and find one that has meant a lot to you personally.
2. Begin to thank the Lord for how He met you in that circumstance and talk to him about how much that part of His character means to you.

Personal Exercise

1. Write down the top 5 ways you have seen God move in your life/family/business.
2. Turn those attributes into a proclamation about who God is to your life/family/business.
3. Pray that proclamation over your family once a week.

Notes:

More Resources

Adoration and Proclamation Prayer Book

This prayer book is a companion to the book, "You Shall Know The Truth" and contains in-depth tools to help you pursue a life of adoration and proclamation prayer.

Includes:
ABC's of Adoration
Who You Are To Me
Proclamation Prayers
Who I Am To You

Available on Amazon and at www.benwoodward.com

Proclamations Audio CD

This CD is music and prayers from the proclamation prayers found in the Prayer book set to music. You can purchase the Mp3's and order physical copies by going to www.benwoodward.com

Discography

Ben Woodward is also a worship leader and songwriter. If you would like to find out more about his music go to: www.benwoodward.com.

These albums are also available on iTunes and at most online music stores.

Adoration App – find it on iTunes